THE
PERFECT
DIAMOND
BUYING GUIDE

THE
PERFECT
DIAMOND
BUYING GUIDE

RICK ANTONA

The Perfect Diamond Buying Guide
© 2021 Rick Antona

Published by LT Press, a division of Longtale Publishing

For information contact:
Uptown Diamond
5151 San Felipe St, Ste 150, Houston, TX 77056

ISBN 978-1-941515-73-0

Book design by Monica Thomas for TLC Book Design
www.TLCGBookDesign.com

Edited by Sharon Wilkerson

Cover photo of Diamonds © cla1978 DepositPhotos.com.

Image contributions by Gemological Institute of America © 2016 GIA: Pg 39 Octaherdral Rough; Pg 70 CAD/CAM software; Pg 71 3D printing; Pg 78 GIA diamond grading report. These images are protected intellectual property and may not be used or reproduced, in whole or in part, without the express, written permission of GIA and other parties as applicable.

Illustrations by KWIRX creative: Pg 31 Diamond Clarity; Pg 42 Carat Weight; Pg 48 Center Stones; Pg 49 Side Stone Shapes; Pg 68 Wedding Ring Stlyes; Pg 55 Lab Grown; Pg 56, 57 Laser Drilling; Pg 59 HPHT Processing; Pg 64-67 Settings.

Interior photos by: Pg 18 Choosing a ring © Agencyby Dreamstime.com; Pg 32 Jeweler loupe © nd3000 Depositphotos.com; Pg 36, 38, 40, 41, 46 Vector diamond shpaes © beaubelle Depositphotos.com; Pg 41 Ruler © dmstudio Depositphotos.com; Pg 70 Wax ring mold photos © Janfaukner Dreamstime.com; Pg 94 Veil © contact@ alexhreniuc.ro Depositphotos.com; Pg 97 Wedding © prostooleh Depositphotos.com; Pg 98 Bouquet © guas Adobestock.com.

CONTENTS

Thank you to Ko-Shin Mandell
for her assistance with this project.
Ms. Mandell was able to comprehend
my goals for this project and help me
organize my thoughts into a format
that is hopefully easy for anyone to
understand and appreciate.

Thank you to Kristina Plunket for

taking the time to read and review

"The Perfect Diamond Buying Guide"
in order to ensure accuracy as to details,
specifications and technicalities related
to diamonds and fine gemstones.

Ms. Plunkett obtained her

GIA Gemologist diploma in 2011 and
subsequently earned her GIA Graduate
Gemologist diploma in 2016.

FOREWORD
BY SEAN JENSEN

DURING THE WINTER OF 2002, I decided to marry my college sweetheart. The first step, a Korean tradition, was to get her father's approval. No problem. The second step, an American tradition, was to buy her an engagement ring. Big problem. I didn't have an older brother to advise me and I was the first amongst my friends to get married. Like most men, I knew nothing about THE ring.

Being the resourceful reporter that I am, I quickly recognized an opportunity to pen an exciting freelance story. My idea was to provide an easy step-by-step, how-to guide for men looking to *put a ring on it*.

I pitched my article idea to a few magazines and inked a deal with the world's largest men's magazine, *Men's Health*.

After pounding the pavement in the Twin Cities, visiting store after jewelry store, I felt increasingly uneasy with the price or the pitch. I just couldn't seem to find a jeweler who I could trust. While researching for my article, I connected with a gemologist and diamond professional 1,176 miles south of my hometown. I was so impressed in our initial phone conversation by Rick Antona's knowledge, passion and professionalism. He never tried to *sell* me anything. His goal was to educate and empower me about how to effectively buy a diamond.

Just like everyone knows someone who has gotten ripped off by a mechanic or duped by a convincing infomercial, most people know someone who has had a bad experience purchasing an engagement ring. Because of this, I knew I needed expert advice.

During our initial chat, Rick provided invaluable tips and suggestions. The very next day I followed his advice at two highly reputable jewelry stores in a posh Minneapolis suburb, but was disheartened to report that I still wasn't comfortable making a purchase.

Rick offered many more ideas and guidance. Finally, in our third conversation, Rick offered to work with me. Ever since that moment, Rick Antona has actually become a part of my family. As someone who was adopted from Korea and didn't grow up with any brothers or sisters, I do not use the word *family* loosely.

In his business, Rick embodies integrity, professionalism, commitment to his products and craftsmanship of the highest order. But what truly distinguishes Rick is that it isn't just *business* to him. The transaction doesn't end the relationship with Rick. He sends thoughtful notes and does regular *check-ins*—not just on the jewelry we've purchased from him but also inquiring about my family's highs and lows. He truly cares.

While my wife Erica and I dated in college, the first jewelry purchase I made for her was a modest gold ring with a small amethyst flanked by two diamond specks. I purchased it from the Post Exchange of the Army base where my parents lived. Even after graduation, Erica wore that ring everyday. It became an extension of her. After we were married, for a special anniversary gift, I had Rick and his team design a much fancier amethyst ring inspired by the original. Erica loved the ring, and unlike her engagement ring or wedding band, which she only showcased on *special occasions*—she wore her new ring daily.

For our 10-year wedding anniversary, we headed to Lake Calhoun in Minneapolis to recreate the signature image of our unforgettable day. It was a picture of me in the lake—in my tuxedo, with my shoes and socks off and pants rolled up—holding Erica in her wedding dress before heading downtown to our reception!

Lake Calhoun was special to us because Erica and I often walked around it, and we had many fond memories there. Erica thought it would be fun to recreate our signature image ten years later with me holding her *and* our two children knee deep in the lake. The picture came off without a hitch, and it is one of our family's favorites. After the photo session, Erica headed to a public bathroom, where she changed our daughter's diaper. The kids had fun at the playground, and then we headed back home. After parking our car, Erica frantically said, "My ring is gone!"

We recounted her steps, and determined the ring must have slipped off while changing our daughter's diaper. I called the Minneapolis Park and Recreation Board and returned to check the bathroom. There was no sign of the ring.

Days later, disappointed and frustrated, I called Rick and asked him to provide a quote to remake that ring. At the time, however, I was in the midst of a career change, and I simply couldn't afford such a luxury. To say the least, I was heartbroken. Four days after our anniversary, I received an unexpected package delivered to my door. I opened the package and discovered it was from Uptown Diamond. Confused, I opened up the box and discovered that it was a new version of Erica's beloved amethyst ring. I was stunned, and Erica was touched. During a period of professional darkness, Rick's gesture was so thoughtful and kind, that it encouraged and inspired me. He didn't backdoor me into a sale, but displayed patience and grace as we later worked out a payment plan I could afford. What Rick did was one of the kindest things anyone has ever done for me. My positive experiences with him have inspired me to refer relatives, friends, famous athletes and business acquaintances, all who report back that they had a stellar experience with him. Because of the countless scams and dishonest practices in the jewelry business, they've all appreciated the connection.

Sitting in my wife's jewelry box, is a diamond ring I purchased for her birthday after we graduated from college (before we were engaged) from a *reputable* jewelry store at the Mall of America. Years later, upon inspection, the diamond has a sizeable crack inside and isn't worth a fraction of what I paid for it.

Let me tell you, Rick Antona is the exception, rather than the rule. I've known him for over a decade now, and I'm grateful for our professional relationship. But even more than that, I am thankful for our personal relationship.

—**SEAN JENSEN**, author of *The Middle School Rules of Brian Urlacher* and former NFL reporter and columnist at the *Chicago Sun-Times, St. Paul Pioneer Press* and *Bleacher Report.*

PREFACE

THERE ARE MOMENTS IN YOUR LIFE that you will never forget ... times that define you and your existence, and somehow bring meaning to our brief human journey. Experiences such as the time when you buy your first car or your first house, or the moment when you purchase a diamond engagement ring to propose to the one person that you've chosen to spend the rest of your life with are everlasting. You will never forget the reaction and the look on your loved one's face when she accepts your proposal and chooses you right back. What girl doesn't remember how her guy proposed to her? That experience is more memorable than *the rock*. Later in life people won't ask you about your ring; they will ask you about the memory of how you were proposed to. These are the truly special and unforgettable treasures of your life.

Unless you have a good jeweler who tells you all about the insider secrets of diamonds, you probably won't buy a great diamond from the start. Most people who buy diamonds don't know anything about them. They just go into a store with their budget and ask for something they can afford, not realizing they bought something potentially worthless until much later in life. When it comes to diamonds, I believe that the average person is not buying anything of true value. I wrote this book as a simple, easy to read guide to help protect you from getting taken advantage of because I know how hard you work for what you have. I want to make sure you get your money's worth. It's just like buying a house. People can rarely afford to purchase their dream home right away. Usually they grow into it over time. Hopefully your investment will be something of value that appreciates over time, so you can continue to build the life you desire.

After reading this book you will have a little bit of ammunition to guard yourself when you go out to buy your first diamond, so that you can actually get value for your hard earned money. If for any reason later in life you decide to upgrade your diamond, or go through financial difficulties and need to cash it in, you will have made an informed purchase to create some financial security for yourself and your loved ones.

*This book could not have been
written without the support of:*

Kerry, Ryan, & Olivia Antona

Ricardo, MaryAnn, & Jennifer Antona

Kevin & Amy Gordon

Alberto Chavez

Jaime "Pops" Garcia

Joseph Delgado

Matthew Fortgang

Craig & Kathy Johnson

Stephen & Galen Reckling

Anthony & Stephanie Milam

Reid and Nicole Ryan

Mace & Melanie Meeks

Jeff Green

Matthew Hall

Melissa Williams

INTRODUCTION

NEVER IN MY LIFE did I think that I would be in the diamond business. My original goal was to attend college, become a physical therapist and work with athletes and professional sports teams. Life has a funny way of changing your direction and turning things around.

After studying at Texas Tech, I had a job managing a fitness studio. I was the guy who got there early, stayed late and made sure that everything was running efficiently. A client named Harry Gordon, Jr. took notice of my attitude and appreciated my work ethic. Even though I had no prior jewelry experience, he asked me to come work for him at Harry Gordon Jewelers. As a young man of 23 who just got engaged and was about to get married, I realized that I needed a good stable job to support my family, so I jumped at the opportunity and dove into the world of diamonds.

While working for Mr. Gordon I learned all about the retail world of diamond and gemstone jewelry, and eventually met my next boss. After joining the team at my next job, I found my true calling when I realized that I wanted to become a gemologist. I took classes with The Gemology Institute of America (GIA) to pursue my official certification and spent the next 21 years working for a prominent diamond cutting house before founding my own business in Houston, Texas.

Now I spend my days (and many nights) at Uptown Diamond working with an incredible team to bring value to some of the most important moments in people's lives.

The secret truth is my big passion has never really been diamonds. What I enjoy most is spending quality time with my clients. I absolutely enjoy getting to know them intimately and helping them make the best decisions on one of the most significant purchases in their life. To me, it's a great feeling, knowing that I have helped make a client very happy. I appreciate being a part of one of the most joyful moments in people's lives and relationships. I enjoy hearing people's proposal stories and seeing photos of their engagement. I find it exciting to be a part of someone's lifelong memories, and I will go out of my way to do anything I can to make that experience the best it can possibly be.

One of the reasons that I knew that I had to write this book was because I wanted to create a guidebook to provide a straightforward explanation about the process of buying a diamond that is simple for anyone to understand. With this book, I want to make sure that when you shop for a diamond, you have the knowledge, resources and tools to make an educated purchase so you ultimately end up receiving the best value for your diamond purchase.

By the time you finish reading this book you will feel comfortable knowing how to choose your jeweler, understand the basics of diamonds, recognize specific necessities before making your purchase, identify the proper documentation, gather a few insider tips and know exactly how to take care of your diamond for years to come.

This book will walk you through the process of designing or discovering the perfect piece of jewelry to bring a world of happiness to your loved one, team member or valued clients and customers.

The objective is to empower you with knowledge and expertise that makes you feel confident when you make important purchases. I hope this book gives you the ability to make the most informed decision possible when purchasing your next lifetime or investment diamond.

CHAPTER ONE

HOW TO CHOOSE YOUR JEWELER

— GETTING STARTED —

A S YOU PREPARE to make a purchase that will last a lifetime, there are several important details you will need to consider in the process of choosing a reputable jeweler. Your first step is to gain as much clarity as possible about the facts regarding your budget, time frame, your loved one's desired diamond shape, ring size, metal and style/setting preferences prior to shopping for your perfect ring. I recommend writing down all of the details you can gather before rushing out the door in search of a jeweler. When it comes to engagement rings, you will encounter an abundance of choices, so the more knowledgeable and prepared you are, the easier it will be to identify the right jeweler and enjoy the process. Remember, this is a once in a lifetime special moment for you! This will be an important part of your most treasured memories for many years to come. It isn't just about buying something beautiful, it's also about your own experiences and the people who get to share the happiest moments of your life with you!

Before we go into the technical details of what to expect from a jeweler you should make sure on a personal level that the people you decide to work with are not only qualified, but kind and trustworthy people with whom you will want to have a long term relationship. Just as you would be careful in choosing a doctor or lawyer, seek out a jeweler who is a professionally trained expert and capable of providing answers in a simple, easy to understand manner. Keep in mind that your ring will need to be taken care of and that most likely you will return to your jeweler many times throughout your life to have it cleaned, inspected or serviced in some way.

Look for a jeweler who has obtained their knowledge from world class, highly reputable certification programs such as the GIA Graduate Gemologist (GG) or the Accredited Jewelry Professional (AJP) Program. Several effective ways to find a great jeweler are: asking family, friends and acquaintances who you trust, searching online and looking for reviews on yelp, researching lists of merchants provided by reputable bridal publications in print or online as well as reading posts by wedding related bloggers. In today's world everyone has a public forum to share their personal experiences on the internet. There is a wealth of information readily available today online. All you need to do is to start looking!

— WHAT TO LOOK FOR —

The average consumer tends to think in brand name extremes recognizing retailers like Costco, Kay Jeweler or Zales on the mainstream end, or the glamorous Tiffany's, Cartier or Harry Winston on the opposite side of the spectrum.

Big name retail jewelers might provide you with a sense of inflated confidence due to their brand recognition, but beware of the old saying: *fast, cheap, and good: pick two.* The concept is that good and cheap service can't be fast, good and fast service won't be cheap and that fast and cheap service just simply is not good. It's a simple phrase to remember when searching for your jeweler. If you want to have everything, expect to pay a bit more.

While buying from a famous store with exceptional quality and service like Tiffany's, Cartier or Harry Winston might seem like an exciting and glamorous white gloved experience, expect to pay significantly more simply because of their name. Aside from a wide range of choices, competitive prices and stellar expertise, there are several additional services and guarantees you should expect from a jeweler as you prepare to make a purchase of this magnitude.

If you purchase your diamond ring from a private jeweler, you can expect to save anywhere from 30–50% compared to traditional retail. Our goal at Uptown Diamond is to provide our clients with the very best quality and the ultimate service, but we are not the least expensive. However, in comparison to Cartier or Tiffany's we are significantly less expensive.

In this book, we will provide you with the information you need to ensure you get a diamond with the best quality and most value for your money. We have included a buying guide in chapter 7 and helpful information on what to do after your purchase in chapter 8. We are also happy to answer any questions you have. Just give us a call at 855-897-5399.

DIAMOND CERTIFICATION

Just like cars have titles and registration, precious diamonds have similar documentation. Before you purchase a diamond, make sure to review its **Diamond Grading Report,** which is a paper that verifies the diamond has been professionally examined by a gemologist and supports the valuation and appraisal of your stone. The report will assure you of the stone's exact qualities and characteristics. All reputable jewelers understand the value of this report and should willingly provide you with this information.

WARRANTIES AND GUARANTEES

As you shop around for the right jeweler, keep your eyes open to the fine print regarding their warranties, return policies and guarantees. In today's competitive market, there's no reason for you to settle for second best. It is 100% possible to find a jeweler who aims to make their clients completely happy. Another important service to seek is a jeweler who provides yearly checkups to inspect and maintain your stone. These annual inspections help your jeweler verify the integrity of your stone, identify any damage or potential issues and ensure that your jewelry stays as beautiful as the day you walked out of the store.

At Uptown Diamond, we stand behind our craftsmanship by offering a lifetime return and exchange guarantee because we believe in providing the best service to our clients. We live by our work and our word.

SAFETY AND SECURITY

When choosing a jeweler, pay attention to the details of how they operate their business. Are they located in a safe environment? Is the building in good condition? Is there adequate security? Uptown Diamond is located at 5151 San Felipe, Suite 150 in the heart of the Houston Galleria Area. We are in the Sage Plaza Building which is a Class A office building. There is 24 hour on site security in the front and back of the building and cameras throughout the perimeter, both outside and inside. Every guest must check in before entering.

DIAMOND HISTORY

EVERY DIAMOND is a one-of-a-kind treasure. There are no two stones exactly alike. Both internally and externally, the world's most coveted and precious stones have unique character-istics that come in many shapes, sizes and colors. The diamond got its name from the Greek word *Adamas* and means *uncon-querable* and *indestructible.* The hardest natural substance found on Earth, a diamond can only be scratched by another diamond. Formed about 100 miles below ground, these beautiful gems have been carried to the Earth's surface by deep volcanic eruptions.

Our planet is roughly 4.5 billion years old, and most diamonds that are found in nature are between one and three billion years old. Over time the sources for discovering the world's most precious stone have changed. Diamonds were first unearthed in India in the 1400s and sold throughout Europe's leading trade centers. Later in the 1700s, Brazil became the leading source of the world's diamonds, until the late 1800s when a massive diamond reserve was discovered in South Africa. Today about half of the world's diamonds originate from Central and South-ern Africa. The other sources are mainly from Australia, Brazil, Canada, India and Russia.

Legend Ancient Greeks and Romans believed that the splinters from falling stars were diamonds. They thought that when the gods cried, their tears were diamonds. The Romans also believed that Cupid tipped his arrows with diamonds. This may have been one of the first of many times that diamonds were associated with love.

CHAPTER TWO

DIAMOND EDUCATION

I N THIS CHAPTER, you will learn about the critical elements that determine the value and worth of a diamond. This will make it easier to ask effective questions of your jeweler. Most often you are buying both a diamond and the setting to hold the stone in place. Make sure to examine the loose un-mounted diamond before selecting the proper setting.

— THE GEMOLOGICAL INSTITUTE of AMERICA —

The Gemological Institute of America (GIA) is a nonprofit institute that was founded in 1931 by Robert M. Shipley as a means to restore the public's faith in the jewelry trade by setting and maintaining standards, then training and certifying jewelers. The GIA developed its International Diamond Grading System based on the Four Cs—a system that is internationally accepted today as a way of assessing the quality of a diamond.

— THE FOUR Cs —

The primary four factors that have been followed for many years in the diamond industry to help determine the value of a finished diamond are known as *The Four Cs*. These notable factors are: Color, Clarity, Cut and Carat Weight/ Size.

THE FOUR Cs
Color: The body color or absence of color
Clarity: The gem's degree of flawlessness
Cut: The stone's proportions
Carat: The weight/size of the gem

Once you understand the four Cs in detail, you will be able to decide what stone effectively combines these qualities together to meet your personal needs.

— #1 COLOR —

One of the first details that most people will notice is the color of a diamond. While the most popular variety of diamonds are transparent white or colorless, diamonds can actually be found in every color of the rainbow. These prominent brightly colored stones are called *Fancy Diamonds* or *Fancies*. The colors range from hues of true yellow and brown as the most common color diamonds, to light blue, light green, pink and lavender in the rare category. Deeper hues of dark blue and green are extremely rare. The most expensive and rare of the fancy diamonds is red.

If you are searching for a white diamond keep in mind that the brighter and whiter the diamond, the better the quality of color and the more expensive it will be.

More than 50 years ago, the GIA established a color grading system to reveal a diamond's colorlessness. This classification system employs an alphabetical scale from the letter D through Z. While the pure and colorless diamond graded D is considered the most desirable and revered color, grades E and F are also extremely rare and priced at a premium.

Most diamonds actually reveal a trace of a yellow or brown tone. The color grading scale shows how the whiter or more colorless diamonds grade higher than diamonds containing a yellowish tint to the stone. The only exception to this is a yellow canary diamond.

GIA COLOR GRADES SUMMARY	D	E	F	G	H	I	J–L	M–Z
	Colorless (Investment Grade)			Near Colorless			Slightly Yellow	Light Yellow

The differences in colorless diamonds can be very subtle from one grade to the next. The layperson will have a challenging time discerning the color grade of a diamond, especially in a stone that is already in a setting. It is very difficult to accurately grade the color of a diamond once it has been mounted.

When you begin to look at diamonds firsthand, you will begin to discover the subtle color differences and gradually gain a greater understanding and appreciation for the different range of prices based on these grades.

THREE WAYS TO MEASURE
THE COLOR GRADE OF A DIAMOND

1. **The Master Set:** The GIA has been building diamond master sets of round brilliant stones with known color grades since the 1950s to aid in the process of color comparison for colorless to light yellow colored diamonds. The carefully maintained diamonds in *The Master Set* range from E-Z.

2. **Colorimeter:** The Colorimeter is an electronic device that was created in Israel in the 1980s. The electronic grader sends a light beam through the stone and a series of filters. A receptor analyzes the beam and then measures the absorption of various colors and generates a reading based on the GIA color grading scale. There is some controversy over the degree to which this

machine is completely effective. The main concern is the difference between the way a human eye sees and interprets color versus the instrument's perspective. Ultimately, gem lab executives agree that the Colorimeter is the best electronic machine grader to date.

3. **The Card Method**: This is a very simple, yet effective method to measure the color grade. Take a pure white business card. Fold it in half. Place the diamond in the crease of the card and view the reflection of color that it gives off. If there is any yellow, the diamond will be lower than grade level K.

HOW FLUORESCENCE FITS INTO COLOR GRADING

Fluorescence in a diamond will show as a soft colored glow when it is put under an ultraviolet light. Around 30% of diamonds will fluoresce to some degree. The D-F colorless fluorescent diamonds sell for up to 15% less since this is perceived as a defect. However, the faint to medium fluorescence visible effects are only recognizable to a gemologist using a UV light source. In the higher grade D-F diamonds, a fluorescence with medium to strong blue can cause the diamond to look cloudy or milky in sunlight. However, in a poorer color grade, the fluorescence actually causes the stone to appear whiter.

To help you remember what to look for, we have a catchy saying at Uptown Diamond: *"None to faint, that's OK! Medium to strong – stay away!"*

HOW COLOR GRADE EFFECTS VALUE

The difference in color grade significantly effects the value of the diamond. Even just a faint presence of color in a diamond can dramatically adjust its value. The value of the same size diamond with a different color grade can widely vary. A simple tip to remember: the less color, the more valuable the diamond.

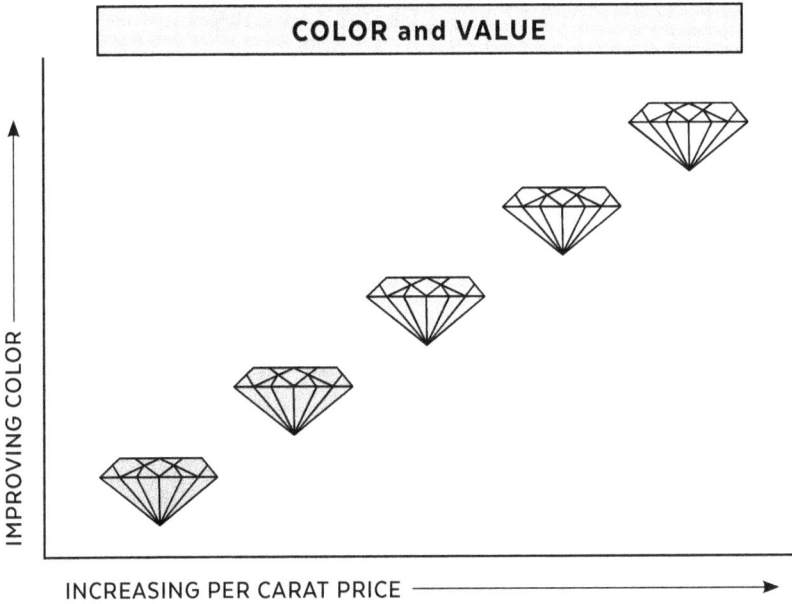

COLOR and VALUE

IMPROVING COLOR →

INCREASING PER CARAT PRICE ⟶

— #2 CLARITY —

Clarity determines how clear and free from blemishes or flaws the gem is when viewed with your own eyes and under a 10x magnification loupe. The cleaner the stone, the rarer the stone will be. This ranking will have a significant effect on the value of a diamond.

In the diamond trade, these internal characteristics are referred to as *inclusions*, an element that was included inside the stone as it was forming in nature.

No two diamonds are alike, each containing its own special internal character and qualities.

External imperfections on the outside of the diamond are called *blemishes* and include chips, pits, bearding, fractures and scratches.

DIAMOND CLARITY FLAWS

The following is a detailed list of possible flaws found in diamonds.

Blemishes (flaws on the outside of the diamond)

1. **Bearding** is a potential blemish on the edges of the diamond in the form of hairline fractures.

2. **Chip** is wear and tear during the cutting process that may cause little pieces of the diamond to fall out.

3. **Extra Facets** effect the proportion and balance of the diamond with extra surfaces that have been polished where they should not have been.

4. **Fracture** larger than bearding, is a true crack on the surface of the diamond.

5. **Natural** is the unpolished parts of the diamond.

6. **Polishing Lines** is a manual mistake where minute lines are created on the diamond during the polishing process.

7. **Scratch** is typically seen as a line on the diamond that tarnishes the smooth surface.

Inclusions (flaws found inside of the diamond)

1. **Cloud:** grouping of spots or pinpoints

2. **Crystal:** included minerals within the body of the host diamond. Crystals can be clear, hazy, colored or black.

3. **Feather:** Feathers are surface reaching inclusions, look like feathers.

4. **Pinpoint:** very small spots or tiny internal dots

5. **Twinning Wisp** is a series of pinpoints, clouds or crystals formed during a diamond's growth produced by an irregularity in the crystal structure, which often appears as a ripple or a wispy line.

BLEMISHES and INCLUSIONS

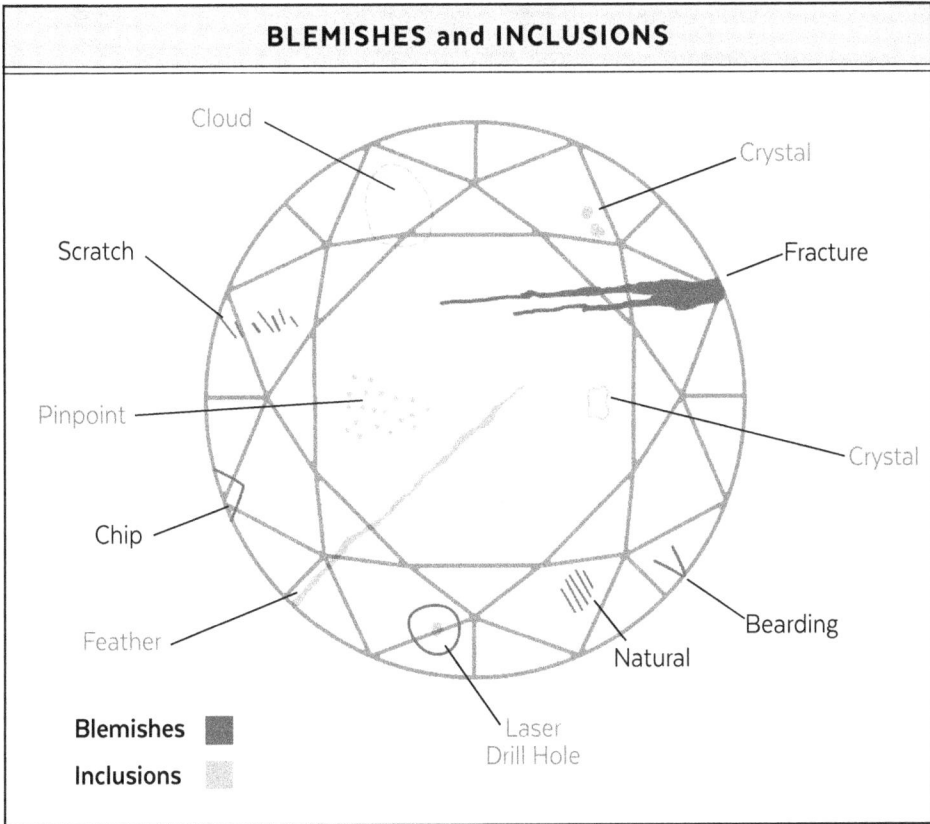

Cloud
Crystal
Scratch
Fracture
Pinpoint
Crystal
Chip
Feather
Bearing
Natural
Blemishes
Inclusions
Laser
Drill Hole

CLARITY GRADES

The GIA has established eleven levels of diamond clarity grades. The grade is based on the number, size, color and location of blemishes or inclusions in the stone.

Even though there are diamonds that are graded as *flawless*— just as in human beings and the world of nature, very few things are actually completely flawless. Most of us tend to think of a flaw as something bad, however a flaw grade in a diamond simply explains and describes a part of the stone's detailed characteristics or personality.

Diamonds are known as the hardest substance in the world, yet they can be scratched by another diamond, and can actually be damaged or chipped through normal wear.

Unless you are a trained professional, you probably won't be able to see the differences in clarity with your own eyes, so it is therefore very important to know the official GIA certified clarity grade of your diamond.

GIA CLARITY GRADES SUMMARY	F	IF	VVS$_1$ VVS$_2$	VS$_1$ VS$_2$	SI$_1$ SI$_2$	I$_1$ I$_2$ I$_3$
	Flawless	Internally Flawless	Very Very Slightly Included	Very Slightly Included	Slightly Included	Imperfect

The following is the GIA Grading Scale:

1. **Flawless:** The most brilliant of all diamonds, free from both blemishes and inclusions. These are the most valuable, rare and costly diamonds.

2. **Internally Flawless:** These diamonds are also amongst the more expensive and rare discoveries for jewelers and clients. They are free from inclusions but may contain slight blemishes on the outside of the diamond.

3. **VVS1 and VVS2 (Very, Very Slightly Included):** These diamonds will have pinpoint blemishes or inclusions and are fairly rare and expensive to purchase.

4. **VS1 and VS2 (Very Slightly Included):** These high quality diamonds will have blemishes or inclusions that are extremely tiny. You will not find any blemish fractures, crystals or breaks in the diamond. (VS1 is the highest clarity you'll have crystals in. At 10x magnification, if you can see an inclusion in 3 dimensional then it's a crystal. At VVS clarity, you'll never have a crystal if the diamond is graded correctly. They can have crystals, but you won't be able to tell they're crystals at 10x. You'd have to bump up the magnification.)

5. **SI1 (Slightly Included):** Great quality diamonds that are *eye-clean,* meaning that they look completely flawless when viewed with the naked eye. Using a loupe you will find tiny inclusions or blemishes that can include carbon and fracture flaws. The SI category includes two grades SI1 and SI2. SI1 is a higher clarity grade than SI2.

6. **SI2 (Slightly Included):** These inclusions may or may not be noticeable to

the naked eye, yet they are visible under a 10x magnification loupe.

7. **I1 (Imperfect):** These are commercial grade diamonds that have very visible blemishes and inclusions that can be seen with the naked eye.

8. **I2 (Imperfect):** This grade will contain diamonds that are cloudy to the naked eye. Inclusions will effect beauty and can effect durability.

9. **I3 (Imperfect):** This is the lowest grade of a diamond. These diamonds are quite unfavorable and contain a great deal of easily visible inclusions and blemishes and can effect durability.

The European Gem Laboratory (EGL) uses an additional diamond grade called the SI3. This diamond is an imperfect stone that would fall under the GIA's I1 grade. It is a clever marketing tool that some jewelers are using to push lesser quality stones.

Diamond Clarity

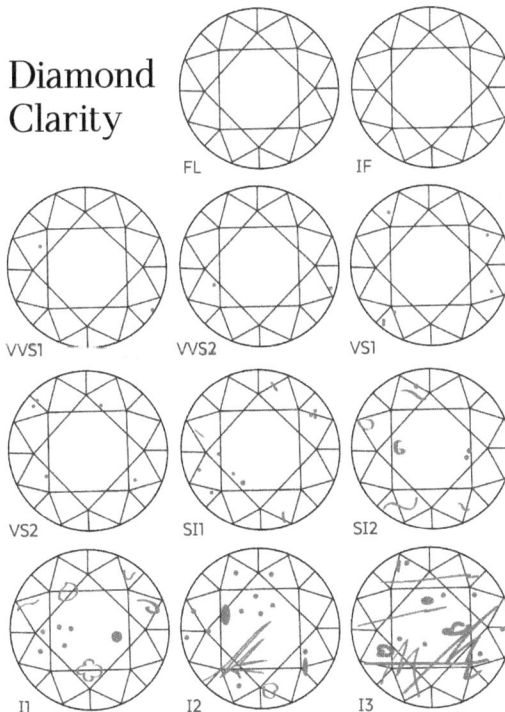

FL

IF

VVS1

VVS2

VS1

VS2

SI1

SI2

I1

I2

I3

Gray marks are inclusions

FTC REQUIREMENTS

The Federal Trade Commission declared that diamond clarity grade must be determined using a minimum 10x magnification scope, also called a loupe. A loupe is a magnifying glass used by jewelers. Most jewelers use a monocular, handheld **loupe** in order to magnify and inspect gemstones or other jewelry. A 10x magnification loupe is the GIA's standard for grading diamond clarity.

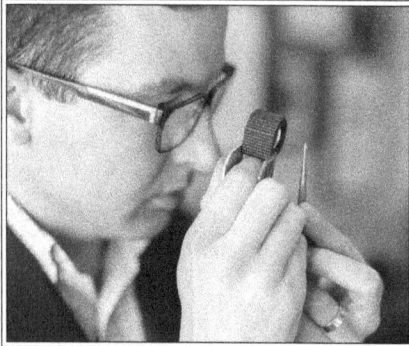

An experienced jeweler will encourage you to view the diamond with a loupe. Any blemishes or inclusions that are not visible with a loupe are not considered in determining the grade and are therefore considered to be nonexistent. If an inclusion or blemish can be seen with the naked eye, it will effect the light passing through the diamond, which in turn effects the sparkle of the stone. Clarity grade has a strong effect on a diamond's ability to sparkle. It is important to note that the FTC allows for one clarity grade and one color grade to be off or misinterpreted in the official diamond clarity grading.

— #3 THE CUT —

The cut of a diamond reveals its brilliance and refers to the finished stone's proportions, symmetry and polish. The beauty of a diamond is fully realized by its cut.

When we speak about cut, it does not refer to the shape. The shape refers to the external perimeter of the diamond. We will cover this aspect in detail later in chapter three.

The cut is the single most important factor in the evaluation of the diamond's finished appearance, and therefore crucial in determining its value. Even if you have a beautiful rough stone that is a perfect colorless diamond of the highest grade, if it isn't cut properly, it won't be considered desirable or exhibit its maximum potential.

Three main effects of the cut are known as:
Brilliance, Fire and Scintillation

- **Brilliance** is the brightness and contrast revealed by the combined reflection of white light from the surface and interior of a polished diamond.

- **Fire** is the flashes of prismatic color created by the dispersion of light.

- **Scintillation** is the amount of intense sparkle a diamond produces, and the pattern of light and dark created as a diamond moves through light.

Diamond cutters are called **lapidarists**. They study a rough diamond very carefully before working on it, with the intention of creating as large and luminous a gem as possible as they cut away at the rough stone. Most diamonds yield between only 40 to 45% from the rough to the polished gemstone, but the price of the polished diamond can increase up to six times as much as the unpolished rough!

DIAMOND CUT PROPORTIONS

The relationship between the size, shape and angle of each of the facets of a cut diamond are known as the proportions. The proportions of a cut diamond have a more powerful impact on a stone's beauty and value than its finish because a rough diamond does not have any sparkle to it at all. It is the alignment and cut of the facets that give a diamond its luminous glow. The ability to cut correct proportions of a rough diamond to realize its most beautiful characteristics is an evolving art form that must be realized with masterful precision.

Diamond grading reports do not fully reveal the specifics about how important characteristics such as color, clarity, faceting, proportioning, transparency and shape unite to create the dynamic beauty of a stone. Your ability to visually assess the appearance of a diamond as you look at it will assist you greatly in discovering what details you prefer. For this reason, it is wiser to purchase your diamond in person than to buy it online or through any other source where you can't touch or see the diamond for yourself.

Joseph Delgado is Uptown Diamond's master diamond buyer based in New York City, and he's traveled the world for over 25 years in search of beautiful gemstones. From India to Israel and Belgium, he has seen more diamonds and gems than most people will ever see in their lifetime.

"Diamonds are beautiful treasures that can be passed down from generation to generation and mark something wonderful," said Delgado. "Nowadays a lot of people are buying their diamonds on the internet based only on what is written in papers and grading reports. When you compare papers, you can have two stones that are a carat each, both H color, SI1, excellent cut, polish and symmetry, but there could still be a big difference in the two diamonds. Labs can make mistakes, and you wouldn't know it just by reading a grading report. If you shop online and just compare what you see written about the gemstone, you are losing the significance of buying a diamond, and you might not get a stone that you love. You are taking the magic out of the experience. I think it's important to find a professional who you can trust to help you find something beautiful and put the romance back into the stone."

The complexities of a diamond's cut cannot be fully appreciated without the eye of an expert guiding you to enjoy firsthand the visual experience of how light moves through a beautifully polished precious diamond. By understanding the architecture of a cut diamond, you will gain insight that will assist you in the search for your perfect diamond. Let's take a detailed look at each of the distinct parts of a cut diamond so you can understand how they work together harmoniously to create a radiantly polished gemstone.

You can look at two stones with the same weight, clarity, color and proportions and one may still be brighter because of the type of raw stone used to cut the stone.

— THE PARTS OF A DIAMOND —

The anatomy of a round, brilliant diamond:

- **The Facets:** Facets are smooth flat planes on the surface of the diamond, which are masterfully cut and carefully positioned to effectively allow light to pass in and out of the diamond, and reflect off its surface at precise angles. This dance of color and light creates the *fire* and *scintillation* that gives a diamond its radiant sparkle.

- **Table:** The table is the largest facet on a diamond located at the flat top where light enters and exits. The size of a table percentage contributes to the amount of brilliance reflected by the diamond.

- **Star Facets:** The star length effects the shape of the table and the angles of the upper girdle.

- **Bezel Facets:** 8 kite-like facets cut into the crown of a round brilliant diamond. Also known as top/main facets and connects the girdle to the table.

- **Upper Circle Facet:** Also known as the *upper halves*, these triangular facets are closest to the girdle edge. There are 16 upper girdle facets.

- **Crown:** This is the part of the diamond between the table and the girdle. The crown splits the light that enters the diamond into white light, creating brilliance and colored light, which creates fire and dispersion.

- **Girdle:** The widest point on a diamond, the girdle protects the edge of a polished diamond from chipping. If the girdle is too thick or too thin it will effect the strength of the diamond.

- **Pavilion:** This is the bottom section of a diamond, below the girdle and above the culet. The pavilion reflects light as it passes through the table and crown. It is composed of a lower girdle, pavilion and optional culet facet.

- **Pavilion Facet:** Kite or diamond shaped, this facet often takes on the appearance of an arrow. There are 8 pavilion facets.

- **Lower Circle Facet:** Also known as *lower halves*, these triangular facets extend from the bottom of the girdle to the culet. There are 16 lower girdle facets.

- **Culet:** Located at the very bottom tip of a diamond, the purpose of this tiny flat facet is to protect the diamond from damage. Diamond settings usually protect the pavilion of the stone from daily impact.

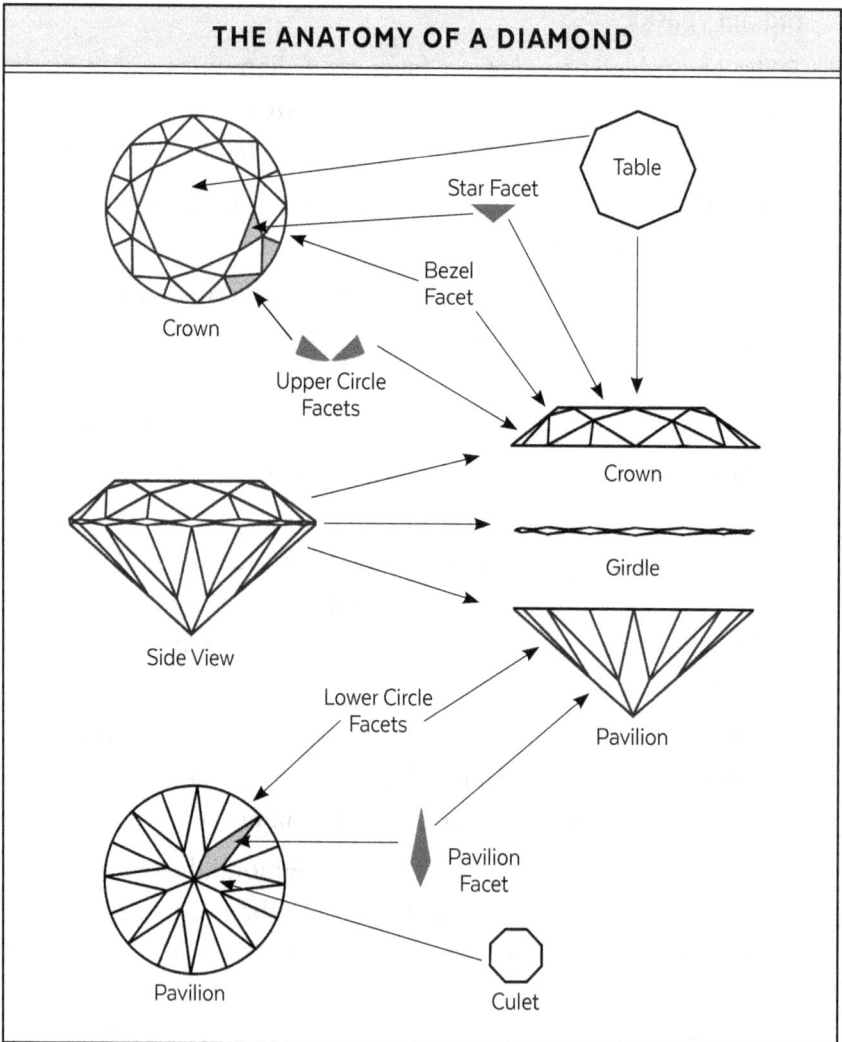

THE ANATOMY OF A DIAMOND

Star Facet

Table

Bezel Facet

Crown

Upper Circle Facets

Crown

Side View

Girdle

Lower Circle Facets

Pavilion

Pavilion Facet

Pavilion

Culet

The white flashes of light emitted from a diamond are known as *brilliance* and the rainbow of colored flashes are called *fire*. The brilliance and fire of a diamond is directly connected to its cut proportions. The relationship between the height of the crown to the depth of the pavilion as well as the relationship between the table facet to the width of the stone are the critical factors that determine and reveal the best characteristics of each polished diamond. When the crown, girdle and pavilion are all cut at the perfect angle and height the resulting harmony creates a diamond that exhibits the maximum fire and sparkle. On the other hand, a poorly cut diamond can make even a highly graded stone look unattractive as well as reduce the value of the diamond by 40–50 percent! Make sure to evaluate diamond brilliance both with the naked eye and a 10x power magnifier from all angles, especially its profile, so you can determine if the proportions of the diamond are balanced. The stones should be viewed below a diffused light source. Never place a diamond under a bare light bulb or spotlight, which can create dark shadows in the stone. It is critical that both the crown and the girdle are not too thick or thin, and that the pavilion isn't too shallow or too deep. A properly proportioned stone will never appear to be very flat or extremely bulky. While every diamond has its own unique symmetry, it's important to consider the alignment of each facet of a diamond's cut, so you can find a stone that sparkles the brightest.

— PROPORTIONS & MEASUREMENTS —

THE IMPORTANCE OF DEPTH PERCENTAGE

Each diamond shape must be cut according to its own specific dimensions in order to reflect the maximum light and display the scintillating fire and sparkle that makes a diamond so magnificent. If the measurements are not carefully calculated and masterfully cut at the correct proportions, the diamond will not live up to its potential, and the result will be reflected in its lack of radiance. By learning the importance of the diamond's depth percentage you will understand the most important characteristics to look for.

Measured in millimeters, the depth of a diamond is the height of the stone from the culet to the table. The total depth percentage is calculated by dividing the total depth of the diamond with the average diameter and then multiplied by 100. The total depth percentage for a round stone should be between 56%–61%.

The *spread* of a diamond refers to how large the stone appears when viewed face up, as you peer into the diamond from the table to the culet. Diamonds with too large of a spread are typically 10% or greater in diameter for round diamonds and 10% or greater in length to width ratio for fancy shape diamonds. If a diamond looks too small or too large for its carat weight, you are most likely looking at a stone that has been inferiorly cut. This occurs when a jeweler cuts the stone for maximum weight and financial profit instead of concern for visual aesthetics, durability and consumer value.

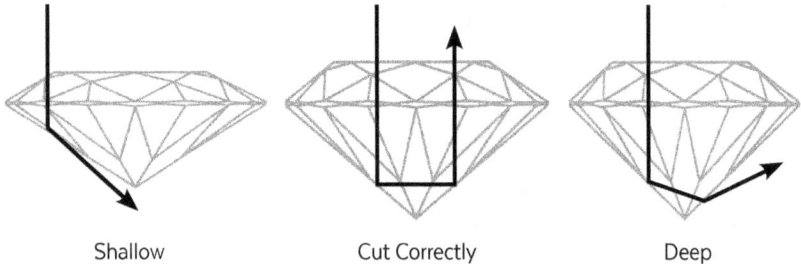

Shallow			Cut Correctly			Deep

A diamond can be cut too shallow in an effort to make the stone seem larger in appearance, but the resulting effect is a diamond that doesn't exhibit its maximum sparkle, along with a few other undesirable traits. A *spread diamond* will measure larger in millimeters (from the left side to right side of the girdle) than another stone of the same carat size, but it will not be as beautiful. Often it will have the unattractive appearance of a fish eye. A spread diamond is thinner at the girdle, the weakest point of a diamond, making it vulnerable to chipping and breakage. While some people might believe it is better to purchase a larger stone, with the false philosophy that bigger means better, the truth is that the diamond's cut has a greater bearing on its visual appearance, quality and financial value.

Another way a diamond cutter tries to maintain the maximum weight from a rough diamond in an effort to gain maximum profit is by cutting the stone too deep. A deeply cut stone appears smaller than an ideal cut diamond of the same carat weight. This is often a result of the demand for larger stones and the increased value of the price of a diamond per carat. Once again, this stone will not exhibit its radiant potential.

THE 65/68 RULE

Most square/rectangular stones are cut with 70/80% table and total depth percentages, which make the stone look smaller and leak a great deal of light, resulting in an unattractive stone. The best proportions for square/rectangular shapes occur when its table percentage doesn't exceed 65% and total depth percentage doesn't exceed 68%. This rule applies to the elegantly cut square and rectangular shaped stones, such as asscher, emerald, princess and radiant cut diamonds.

THE ROUGH DIAMOND

When diamonds are in their natural untouched state, they are called roughs. Rough diamonds have been discovered in a wide variety of shapes, sizes and colors, with each stone containing its own beautiful unique characteristics that yield varying results.

The shape of a rough diamond determines the possible shape of a cut diamond. Though diamonds are cut to retain their weight, a rough diamond will lose between 40-70% of its weight during the cutting process.

The price of two similarly cut stones of the same size can vary greatly depending on the quality of the rough diamond prior to being cut and polished. While most people would think it was the polished stone that determines a diamond's value, it is actually *the rough diamond* that bears more importance on the value of the gemstone.

A flat piece of rough diamond has a collapsed crystalline structure, which will therefore effect the way light moves through the stone in comparison to other rough shapes.

The shape that produces the best results is the octahedral rough. These gemstones formed in the earth at precisely the perfect temperature and pressure and allow light to enter and exit the diamond in a harmonious flow that reveals the maximum radiance and sparkle. Octahedral roughs produce more beautiful stones than other rough diamond shapes and consequently, finished diamonds from octahedral roughs are the most expensive diamonds.

Length To Width Ratio

The relationship of a cut diamond's proportions is known as the length to width ratio. By dividing the length of the diamond with its width, you obtain the length to width ratio. This is especially relevant for fancy cuts such as asscher, pear, radiant, princess, marquise, emerald, cushion, oval, and heart shaped diamonds.

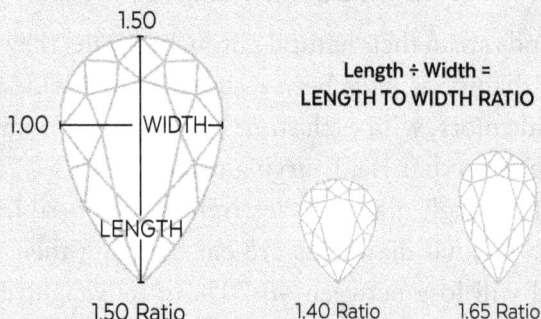

1.50

1.00

WIDTH

LENGTH

Length ÷ Width =
LENGTH TO WIDTH RATIO

1.50 Ratio   1.40 Ratio   1.65 Ratio

Examining the shape's length to width ratio helps to determine the symmetry and perfection of the cut gem.

—#4 CARAT—

WHAT IS A CARAT?

Diamonds are sold by the carat. A carat is a unit of weight used for diamonds and other gemstones. It is important to note that weight does not refer to size. One carat is divided into 100 points. Therefore, 1ct = 1.00, ½ ct = .50. A jeweler will often describe a diamond that weighs less than one carat by its point value. For example; a diamond that weighs .25 carats as a 25 pointer or ¼ carat. Another example: 0.33 carats is expressed as ⅓ of a carat or as 33 points.

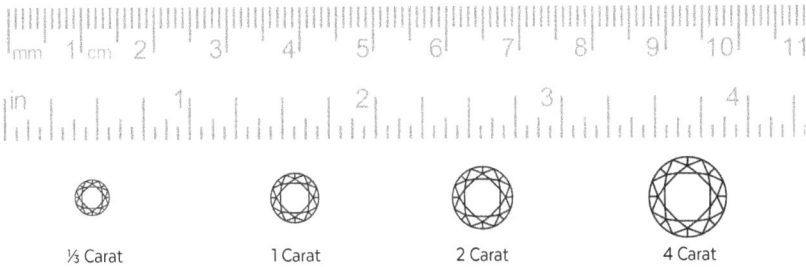

| ⅓ Carat | 1 Carat | 2 Carat | 4 Carat |

WHY IS CARAT WEIGHT IMPORTANT?

Carat weight is a significant factor in determining the price of a diamond. A general rule would be that as carat weight increases, so does the value. The other factors that make up the 4Cs: color, clarity and cut—all combine together to effectively determine the value of two diamonds of equal carat size. Large diamonds are much rarer in nature than smaller ones and their rarity to value ratio is priced accordingly. Less than one in a million mined rough stones are capable of producing a beautifully finished one carat diamond.

SIZE VERSUS CARAT WEIGHT

As we discussed previously, carat is a unit of weight/mass. Size refers to the dimensions measured in millimeters (mm). Depending upon its depth, a one-carat round brilliant diamond can range from 6.20 mm to 6.80 mm in diameter. The *spread* of a diamond refers to the visual appearance of the stone's size, based on its diameter. A jeweler may describe that a stone has a spread of one carat. Please note: it does not weigh one carat! The diamond will appear to look like a one-carat stone. The size of your diamond can be visually aided or impaired by the way in which your stone is cut. A thick stone will appear smaller in diameter than a stone that is cut shallow.

CARAT WEIGHT	0.25	0.5	0.75	1	1.5	2	3	4
Round								

WHAT CARAT WEIGHT IS RIGHT FOR ME?

In order to determine the perfect carat weight of your diamond, you should consider the following:

1. What is the size of the recipient's finger? *The smaller the finger and hand, the larger the diamond will appear. A one carat diamond looks much larger on a size 5 finger than on a size 8.*

2. What kind of setting have you chosen? *The shape of the diamond is an important factor in choosing a compatible setting. If you need help determining which setting is perfect for your stone shape, we are always available to help you at Uptown Diamond. Just call our offices in Houston at 855-897-5399 and we will be happy to answer any of your questions.*

3. What is your budget? *If the carat weight is a top priority, yet you are working with a strict budget, we recommend a well cut diamond in the shape of your choice, SI1-SI2 Clarity Grade, and a color grade of I or J.*

Did you know that the term **"carat"** is derived from the Greek word "keration" which means fruit of the carob? Native to Mediterranean regions, Carob trees produce delicious edible pods with seeds that are all uniform in size, which was useful for traders back in ancient times who used the seeds to balance a scale as they weighed precious gemstones.

CHAPTER THREE

CLASSES OF DIAMONDS

THE IDEAL CUT DIAMOND (CLASS I)

THE IDEAL CUT round brilliant diamond has 58 facets symmetrically placed to produce the ultimate radiance and beauty. The ideal proportions allow the light that enters from any direction to be reflected back out through the table (the top of the diamond) and expand out into a rainbow of glowing colors and flashes of sparkle.

GIA CLASS 1		
Total Depth	59.3% – 61.0%	Megascope/Sarin
Table Percentage	53.0% – 60.0%	Megascope/Sarin
Crown Angle	34.0° – 35.0°	Megascope/Sarin
Crown Height	13.5% – 16.2%	Megascope/Sarin
Pavilion Angle	42.2° – 41.2°	Megascope/Sarin
Pavilion Depth	42.5% – 43.6%	Megascope/Sarin

(Continues on next page)

(GIA Class 1 continued)

Girdle Thickness	Thin – Slightly Thick
Polish & Symmetry	Excellent – Very Good
Fluorescence	None – Faint

THE PREMIUM CUT DIAMOND (CLASS II)

A Premium Cut diamond succeeds in creating a balance and harmony between its proportions. The result of this cut is a beautiful display of brilliance as the diamond reflects the light.

GIA CLASS 2		
Total Depth	56.0% – 61.0%	Megascope/Sarin
Table Percentage	53.0% – 64.0%	Megascope/Sarin
Crown Angle	32.0° – 35.0°	Megascope/Sarin
Crown Height	11.2% – 16.2%	Megascope/Sarin
Pavilion Angle	40.0° – 41.5°	Megascope/Sarin
Pavilion Depth	42.3% – 43.9%	Megascope/Sarin
Girdle Thickness	Thin – Thick	
Polish & Symmetry	Excellent – Good	
Fluorescence	None – Faint	

THE INFERIOR CUT DIAMOND (CLASS III AND IV)

When light enters through the table of an ideal cut diamond, it radiates its glow through each and every facet. The issue with inferior cut or poorly cut diamonds is they were cut to retain the maximum weight of the original rough diamond. In doing that, they forfeit their potential fire and brilliance. Whether they are top heavy or too shallow, these diamonds suffer from an imbalance that does not effectively allow light to circulate through the stone to create the most desirable sparkling effect. The variety of results of *Inferior Cut* diamonds can include a stone that looks dark in the center or appears murky, glassy and watery.

GIA CLASS 3		
Total Depth	61.1% – 64.5%	Megascope/Sarin
Table Percentage	65.0% – 70.0%	Megascope/Sarin
Crown Angle	30.0° – 31.9°	Megascope/Sarin
Crown Height	6.5% – 11.1%	Megascope/Sarin
Pavilion Angle	41.6° – 43.1°	Megascope/Sarin
Pavilion Depth	43.9% – 45.5%	Megascope/Sarin
Girdle Thickness	Very Thin – Very Thick	
Polish & Symmetry	Good – Fair	
Fluorescence	None – Medium	

GIA CLASS 4		
Total Depth	64.6% or more	Megascope/Sarin
Table Percentage	71.0% or more	Megascope/Sarin
Crown Angle	29.9° and below	Megascope/Sarin
Crown Height	6.4% and below	Megascope/Sarin
Pavilion Angle	43.2° or more	Megascope/Sarin
Pavilion Depth	45.5% or more	Megascope/Sarin
Girdle Thickness	Extremely Thin – Extremely Thick	
Polish & Symmetry	Fair – Poor	
Fluorescence	None – Very Strong	

— NEGATIVE CUTTING EFFECTS —

Diamonds that are poorly cut will negatively effect the appearance of a potentially luminous stone. When a diamond is cut too shallow or too deep, it reduces the amount of light the stone emits. These negative effects resemble inclusions and severely reduce the diamond's value. No matter what grade the diamond is, these unwanted effects detract from the gem's beauty, decreasing their sparkle and brilliance.

FISH EYE

This is an unwanted effect that occurs when a diamond is cut too shallow, the girdle is too thick or the table facet is too large. It appears as an unattractive grey circle or ring, right in the center of the stone. It looks just like a fish eye, and is considered to be a severe flaw.

NAIL HEAD

When the pavilion of a diamond is cut too deep, an unattractive large dark circle appears in the center of the stone. This is called the nailhead effect, and it will make a beautiful diamond appear dark and lifeless.

BOW TIE

A bow tie is the presence of a shadow in the center of a poorly proportioned cut diamond. The shadow appears smaller in the center of the stone and widens as it reaches the perimeter of the diamond, in the shape of a bow tie. This optical effect is directly linked to its make or inferior cut. The stones most readily affected by the bow tie effect are fancy cuts, such as oval, marquise, emerald and pear shaped diamonds. Although the faint appearance of a bow tie like shadow is expected in these fancy cuts, a prominent grey to black bow tie is considered to be a very undesirable characteristic.

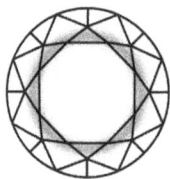 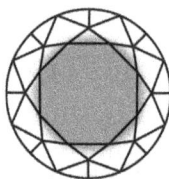 

Fish Eye   Nail Head   Bow Tie

A word of caution for anyone considering purchasing a diamond online: be aware that these effects will not be mentioned in a diamond grading report.

— SHAPES —

Today there are many beautiful shapes and cuts to enjoy. The style of cut can have a slight effect on the value. When pricing diamonds it's easiest to compare stones of the same shape. The shape of a diamond has been said to reveal a great deal about someone's personality. Although factors such as price and quality are important when purchasing a diamond, it would be wise to consider what the recipient of the diamond would appreciate the most.

CHOOSING THE BEST SHAPE

The round brilliant diamond is the most popular style, known for having a perfectly symmetrical arrangement of facets and proportions that have been mathematically calculated. The round brilliant represents over 75% of all diamonds sold today. Additionally, there is a wide variety of other magnificent shapes. Each has its own benefits and beauty. The shape you choose will have an effect on the amount of brilliance and sparkle of the diamond. If you are considering how big you want your diamond to appear, the oval, pear and marquise shapes tend to look larger than their carat weight in comparison to other cuts.

Most people have a preference for the shape they would like. For an engagement ring, it is possible that your partner-to-be has spent many years dreaming of the day when the love of her life proposes. They might even have collected images of rings that they wish were their own. If you wanted this engagement to be a surprise, speaking privately to family members or friends who know your partner well could help you decide what shape to choose. One last important factor in choosing the best shape of your diamond is the size and proportion of the recipient's hand.

THE TOP TEN MOST POPULAR CENTER STONE SHAPES

Round

Oval

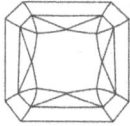

Box Radiant

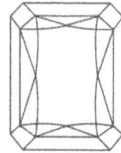

Standard Radiant

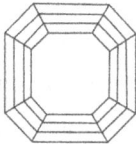

Asscher

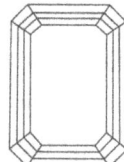

Emerald Cut

Pear

Marquise

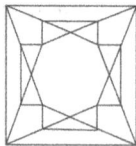

Princess

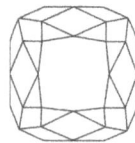

Cushion

THE TOP TWELVE MOST POPULAR SIDE STONE SHAPES

Straight Bullet

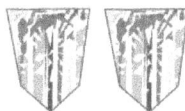

Taper Bullet

Pear

Heart

Half-Moon

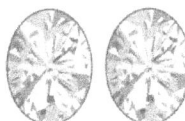

Oval

Brilliant Trapezoid

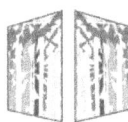

Step Trapezoid

Shield

Trillion

Round

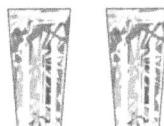

Tapered
Baguettes

CHAPTER FOUR

TREATMENTS & SYNTHETICS

Y EARS AGO, most diamonds sold in stores were natural and untreated. Due to the demands of the current marketplace, as well as the increasing capabilities of new technologies, this is no longer an assumption you can make. There are now a variety of ways that diamonds are being treated, enhanced or produced in laboratories. Treatment status can significantly alter the value of a diamond. When shopping for a diamond, remember to ask if the color and clarity of a stone are natural or the effect of a treatment.

In this chapter, we will discuss several methods of treating and producing diamonds. These treatments are virtually indistinguishable to the untrained eye. Always remember to check if the diamonds you are viewing are untreated and accompanied by grading reports. Any alteration of a diamond through a human generated process, other than cutting, cleaning or polishing results in a stone that is considered to be a treated stone. When purchasing a diamond, remember that untreated diamonds are in demand, enhanced diamonds are not and therefore have very low resale potential.

IS IT REAL?
— SYNTHETIC vs. NATURAL —

The definition of synthetic becomes important in regards to diamonds. While one definition means fake or not real when referring to mineralogy or jewelry, synthetic takes on a completely different meaning. Synthetic in regards to diamonds or gemstones notes that the mineral was man-made to be physically, chemically, and optically identical to its counterpart found in nature. As an example let's use ice. If I need ice for my drink I have a couple of options to get it. I can go to the Antartic and chisel a piece of ice from a glacier where it formed under situations found in nature. Or I can put some water in a cup and put it into my freezer. both are ice, but one formed in nature while the other was man-made. Synthetics are created in laboratories and depending on the production method, are categorized as CVD diamonds (chemical vapor deposition), or HPHT diamonds (high-pressure, high-temperature). Both CVD and HPHT diamonds can be cut into gems of a variety of colors including clear white, brown, blue, green, orange and yellow.

With synthetics on the rise, the gemological labs carefully test each diamond in order to determine if the gem is natural or man-made. If the diamond is found to be synthetic, the GIA laser-inscribes the girdle of the stone with a report number, releases a statement that the diamond has been grown in a laboratory and issues an official document entitled *The Synthetic Diamond Grading Report*. It is important to note that you will probably not be able to tell the difference between a lab-grown diamond and a naturally mined one. Regarding cost, synthetic diamonds retail for approximately 30-40% less than mined diamonds.

DIAMOND SIMULANTS

Unlike lab-created diamonds that consist of real carbon atoms that are specifically arranged in the crystalline structure of geologically grown natural diamonds, the reality is that diamond simulants are just diamond look-alikes. They are not true carbon crystals. Diamond simulants have similar gemological characteristics to diamonds, but are not considered to be synthetic diamonds. Cubic zirconias, moissanites, and high-leaded glass (rhinestones) are classified as *diamond simulants*.

HOW TO DETECT A FAKE DIAMOND

Below you will find some simple, yet effective methods to test whether or not a stone is a real diamond. After you have done your own tests, consult a qualified gemologist to have an official analysis of your stone.

1. View the Diamond Through a Loupe
   - A fake diamond will look absolutely perfect.
   - Naturally grown gemstones will reveal imperfections in the form of carbon.
   - A real stone will have sharp edges, whereas a fake one will have rounded edges.
   - If the diamond is in a setting, take note of the metal used. Most diamonds are mounted in gold or platinum.

2. Sandpaper Test
   - Real diamonds are one of nature's hardest substances and can't be scratched by the rough surface of sandpaper.
   - If it scratches, it's most likely a cubic zirconia.

3. See-Through Test
   - Looking at the stone face up, can you can see through it? If you can, it is probably not a real diamond.
   - Put the stone face down on top of a newspaper—if you can see the print below, it is most likely a fake.

4. The Fog Test
   - Real diamonds do not retain heat.
   - Breathe hot air onto your stone—A diamond will fog but clear very quickly (within a couple of seconds) where a simulant will stay fogged for a much longer period. This has a lot to do with humidy and temperature of the environment as well.

5. Rainbow Sparkle Test

  ◆ Hold the stone in the light and see how it sparkles.

  ◆ Does it give off a rainbow colored glow? It is probably a fake!

  ◆ Real diamonds give off a grey or white sparkle known as brilliance.

6. Price Test

  ◆ Is the price too good to be true? It could be an imitation diamond, or perhaps defective or stolen merchandise.

7. Thermal Conduction Test

  ◆ A GIA GEM Pocket Thermal Tester is a tool to quickly and easily determine if a stone is an imitation. This tool measures the heat conductivity of a stone by pressing a metal probe of the pen onto the stone. The instrument then provides a reading of either *diamond* or *imitation*.

— IF IT'S NOT A DIAMOND, WHAT IS IT?! —

The following are some colorless stones that mimic or emulate the look of a diamond. These stones are often used to imitate real diamonds:

Cubic Zirconia: Made of zirconium oxide, these are low cost, durable, optically flawless diamond simulants that have been synthetically grown and mass-produced since 1976. These stones are easily scratched and lack the fire and scintillation of a natural diamond.

White Topaz: A variation of the naturally occurring silicate mineral, topaz is usually a colorless gemstone that is often tinted by impurities and appears in many colors. Some stones may have easily visible inclusions and scratch quite easily. This natural gem tends to have a glassy appearance.

White Sapphire: Known as corundums, these beautiful stones come from the same gemological family as blue sapphires and rubies. The white sapphire is a rare and geologically grown precious gem. Considered to be the one of the strongest gems on Earth (second to the diamond) the white sapphire is only a quarter as durable as a diamond. In comparison to diamonds, white sapphires are easily scratched or chipped, and lack the radiant fire and luminous sparkle that a beautiful diamond displays. Synthetic white sapphires are also available in the marketplace, but they are not nearly as durable as natural sapphires.

Moissanite: Discovered in 1893 by a scientist examining meteor samples in Arizona, this is a gem that contains almost all of the same qualities of a diamond. Having thought he discovered a diamond, it was later reported to be a very rare gem that is now grown in laboratories and sold for a fraction of the cost of diamonds. *Please note: the difference between a diamond and moissanite is practically indistinguishable to the naked eye, even under a microscope. A trained gemologist uses a special tool to determine if the stone is a diamond or moissanite.*

Lab Grown: Carefully created in highly controlled lab environments, these cultured diamonds are cultivated using state-of-the-art advanced technology that replicates the conditions under which natural diamonds are formed in the earth. Lab diamonds are grown from small carbon seeds of pre-existing natural diamonds. After they are grown, they are carefully cut and polished in the same manner as a geologically grown diamond obtained through mining. They are available as colorless or fancy colored diamonds.

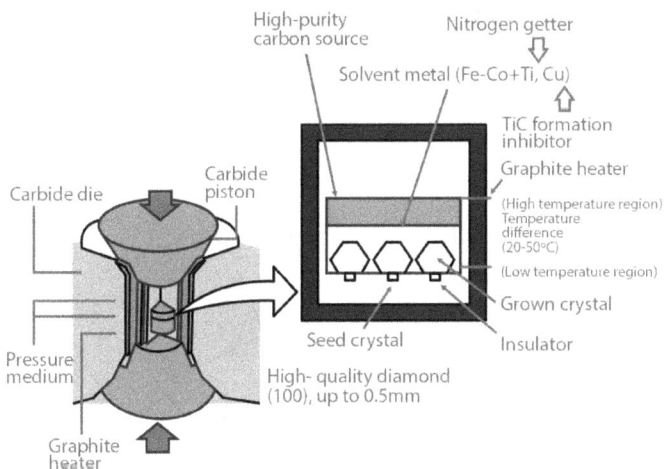

Man-made diamonds are indistinguishable from naturally formed diamonds. All diamonds available for purchase should come with lab grading reports and certification that identifies your diamond as either a natural diamond or lab grown.

ENHANCEMENTS TO
— NATURAL DIAMONDS —

There are currently a variety of high-tech treatments performed on natural diamonds that have been cultivated to improve the visual characteristics of cut and polished diamonds. From clarity treatments to laser drilling, fracture filling, coatings, irradiation and heating, it is now possible to enhance and improve the quality of diamonds. Though the appearance of treated diamonds is radically improved, this is a controversial subject as many professionals dispute the purity of performing these enhancement processes on natural diamonds. All enhancement treatments should be disclosed to potential consumers, as they can require special care, and have a significant effect on the diamond's value.

LASER DRILLING

Laser drilling is a type of clarity enhancement introduced by General Electric in the late 1960s. This permanent treatment is designed to remove and significantly reduce the appearance of microscopic

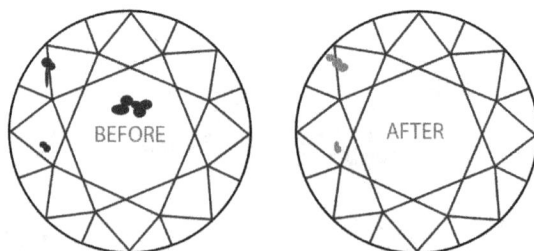

Before and after image of a laser drilled diamond

black carbon inclusions. An infrared laser beam is used to drill very fine holes into the dark area(s) of the gem. After the gem has been drilled, the holes that reach the surface are invisible to the naked eye. Under a microscope or a 10x loupe, a laser-drilled area can be seen as a tiny white dot when examining the diamond face up, and a thin white line

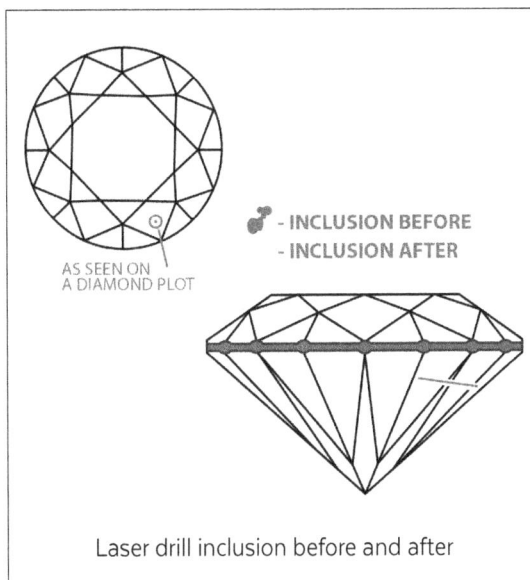

AS SEEN ON
A DIAMOND PLOT

- INCLUSION BEFORE
- INCLUSION AFTER

Laser drill inclusion before and after

when viewed from the side of the stone. Focused only on the effected area, laser drilling does not change the internal characteristics of the rest of the diamond, nor does it add a foreign substance into the stone. Additionally, laser drilled diamonds are not damaged by normal cleaning, repairs or daily wear.

FRACTURE FILLING

Fracture filling is a diamond treatment that enhances both clarity and transparency and is used to conceal feathers (or fractures) in diamonds. The process involves injecting a glass-like substance into these narrow fractures or cracks. The result is usually invisible to the naked eye. This controversial technique is often discussed as being unstable, as it can be a non-permanent treatment. Though it is reportedly a durable process, some conditions could cause the filled treatments to become damaged, melt or alter the diamond's tone. Extended exposure to UV radiation/sunlight can possibly cause these fillings to discolor. Fracture filling can be a quite subtle enhancement and requires a skilled diamond grader to identify its presence.

— COLOR ENHANCEMENTS —

COATINGS

In order to improve a diamond's color grade, occasionally stones are visually enhanced by a coating. This is a non-permanent process that is considered to be a deceptive trade technique. Coatings can include dyes, films and other chemical compounds used to mask the true color of a stone. One of the most ambiguous treatments is applying a thin film of synthetic diamond to the surface of a diamond simulant to give it many of the characteristics of a real diamond. Though it can be difficult to detect, a trained professional can identify coatings with magnification, color filters and solvents.

IRRADIATION

Irradiation is a high-energy process that physically alters the diamond's crystalline structure to create new concentrations of color. Light yellow and brown diamonds have been transformed through irradiation to yield blue, green, yellow, black, dark green, orange, pink, purple and red colored diamonds. In general, the color tones of irradiated diamonds are stable. The benefit of this color treatment is that these diamonds are sold at a fraction of the cost of their natural counterparts, but they are very difficult to resell if you are considering them as an investment purchase.

HEATING – HPHT

HPHT stands for high-pressure, high-temperature. This is a highly effective, virtually undetectable diamond treatment that was first employed in the 1970s to alter the color of diamonds to yellows and greens. Around 1999, General Electric discovered that it was possible to transform inexpensive brown diamonds into valuable colorless ones with this process. By applying temperatures up to 2,000 degrees Celsius, and pressures of up to 70,000 atmospheres, HPHT is a technique capable of radically transforming the color of certain diamonds. Through the HPHT process, some diamonds are transformed to a more desirable color tone. Brown diamonds can become light yellow, greenish-yellow and yellowish-green. Higher color graded diamonds have been transformed to white, blue-ish grays and even become colorless.

Treated diamonds have a much lower resale value and are not the best option for investment diamonds.

Some synthetic diamonds have been HPHT treated to visually alter their properties, thus making it more difficult to differentiate them from natural diamonds. These treatments can also effect the toughness of the stone and make it less resistant to scraping, scratching and chipping from normal wear. It is important to weigh the benefits and shortcomings of treated diamonds when considering your purchase.

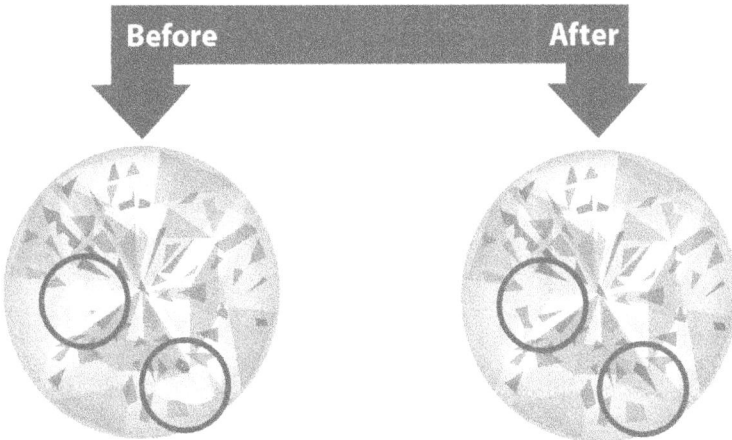

Before and after HPHT Processing

CHAPTER FIVE

SETTING & STYLE

W HETHER IT'S AN engagement ring or a special gift for a loved one, choosing the right setting for your ring should enhance the look of your diamond. Most jewelers offer a wide variety of settings and styles, and if you are lucky you might find a jeweler capable of making your own truly spectacular one-of-a-kind custom design.

Once you have chosen your perfect diamond, the three key elements of designing a ring are: choosing the desired metal, selecting the perfect setting for your beautiful stone and picking the ring size. Most people may feel challenged by all of the different choices available, and some have a very difficult time making a decision at this stage, yet this is actually the most fun part of choosing a ring! Although the diamond itself will often make up for approximately 80-90% of the ring's cost, it is the actual setting that fully showcases and expresses the diamond's exquisitely polished beauty. In this chapter we will discuss the various options for your metal type and setting.

— PERSONAL STYLE —

As you consider the setting and style for your fiancée's ring, it is important to think about their specific personality. It is just as important to look at the types of metals your loved one wears and the jewelry they currently own, in addition to their personality. How would you define their sense of style? Are they understated, traditional, classic, modern, romantic, sophisticated, glamorous, earthy, or edgy and bold? Is this a person who would want to show off their ring to everyone they meet, or someone who is more private and prefers to keep their personal effects to themselves? How do they use their hands everyday? What is their lifestyle and what kind of hobbies and activities/sports do they enjoy? Do they spend time with children or fine fabrics? A person who works with their hands all day might prefer a ring that's more simple and practical to one that's big and flashy or very fancy. Take notice of what kinds of designers they already appreciate in fashion and accessories, as well as their daily wardrobe. Is this someone who stays on top of the latest fashion trend or a timeless classic?

Some other important elements to consider are hand size and shape, as well as skin tone. These are all small, yet very important details to gather as you make your decision and select the perfect metal and ring setting for your loved one. Though ultimately, personal preference is more important than trends or fashion.

— CHOOSING A METAL —

As you decide on the type of precious metal for the ring, a helpful hint is to look at the most often worn jewelry of your loved one. This will help you to learn their preference, especially if you want the ring to be a surprise. When in doubt, ask someone who is close to your loved one to help you make the best choice.

The most popular metals for engagement rings are platinum, 18 karat and 14 karat gold. Karat gold is measured strictly in units of 24, therefore 24k gold is 100 percent pure gold. Pure gold is too soft to use for jewelry, and in order to increase its durability it is mixed with other metal alloys. Platinum is one of the rarest metals on earth. It is much more durable than gold, in turn more expensive. Made of 95% pure platinum and 5% metal, it retains its color for life, making platinum a very dependable choice. Additionally, if you are concerned about allergies, this durable yet solid metal is perfect because it is completely hypoallergenic and very rarely causes skin reactions. Platinum rings are also very easy to take care of and only require light cleaning and polishing. 18k gold is not as strong as platinum, yet still very durable and resistant to scratching. If your budget is an important factor, you will find that 18k gold is less expensive than platinum. 18k gold is comprised of 75% pure gold and 25% alloys and can be found in three distinct tones: yellow gold, white gold or rose gold. 14k gold is composed of 58.3% gold and 41.7% other metals and is one of the more popular gold choices in the United States. Platinum and white gold have a luminous silvery hue. Gold has a distinctly yellow tone, and rose-gold reflects a lovely pink/rose hue. Because of its yellow tone, yellow gold can make a slightly yellowish or brownish diamond look colorless in comparison. It is often chosen for this reason, as well as personal taste and preference.

It is important to note that while 14k and 18k white gold is an extremely popular choice, it is usually plated with another metal called rhodium that adds the luminous sheen to its finish. In order to maintain this lustrous and bright finish over time, all white gold must be periodically re-plated with rhodium or unfortunately it will not maintain its beauty. Rose gold finishes have a very contemporary edge to them. They somehow evoke a distinctly classic vintage yet timeless style. Rose gold is created using an alloy mix and does not exist in the natural world. Though rose gold is considerably more durable than yellow or white gold, because it is mixed with copper alloys, it is not considered to be hypoallergenic. On a very positive note, rose gold is surprisingly affordable, does not require rhodium plating, and is quite flattering on all skin tones. In addition to gold and copper, rose gold can have silver or zinc mixed within, so it would be important to consider any types of metal allergies the ring's recipient could experience before choosing rose gold for your metal.

— SELECTING THE SETTING —

The following are considered to be the most popular styles of today:

PRONG

Prong settings are the most common engagement ring settings that involve three to six prongs to firmly hold the stone in place. There are a variety of prong styles including pointed, rounded, flat and V-shaped. This beautiful style allows the greatest light exposure from all sides of the diamond and truly emphasizes the diamond's fire and brilliance. Prong settings are very easy to clean. Due to their exposed girdle, this setting offers less protection to the stone than other styles, and can easily scratch a person, get caught in clothing and are difficult to fit in gloves. Prong settings use less metal and are often less expensive than other styles.

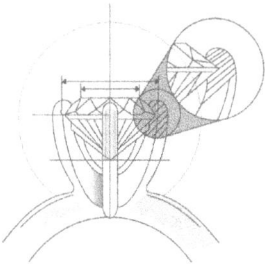

BEZEL

This is considered to be the second most popular setting style because of its modern look and durability. Bezel settings surround the stone with a metal rim that extends slightly above the stone, encircling the center stone tightly in place. This is a very secure, protective setting that is perfect for anyone with a very active lifestyle as this setting completely embraces the girdle and pavilion of the diamond. The only real disadvantage of this setting is less light is capable of passing though the ring, making it appear to have less luminosity and sparkle.

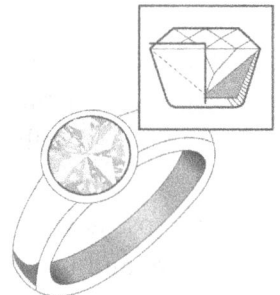

CHANNEL

Extensively used for wedding bands, this popular setting places a number of smaller stones together in a continuous row. It is possible to completely surround the ring with stones and this style is often used to accent large center stones. Channel settings are considered to be extremely contemporary and very fashionable. Depending on the craftsmanship of this ring, it is possible for stones to fall out if they do not each have an individual pocket or seat within the ring.

PAVÉ

Pavé settings employ a grouping of multiple small stones set together in a cluster where little metal shows through to give the impression of a completely paved cobblestone-like path of diamonds. The stones are commonly round or square and are expertly fitted side-by-side on the surface of the ring. Pavé settings are usually used in conjunction with other settings to enhance the beauty of the large center stone creating a glimmering, shimmering border. One of the benefits of a pavé setting is that the glimmer of the lustrous setting is so beautiful that it can help boost the look of a center stone that might not radiate as much fire.

FLUSH

This technique describes highly precise, intricately placed stones with multiple tiny prongs like little frames, that carefully hold each stone in place. Compared to other settings, this type has a greater chance of the stones falling out during regular daily wear.

BAR

This beautiful contemporary, yet classic setting is slightly similar to the channel setting. The channel settings enclose the diamond on all sides, whereas bar set diamonds allow the diamond to be exposed on two sides by holding the stones in place with metal bars. It is used in a circular band, and can also be used to compliment a larger center stone.

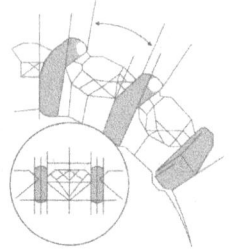

BEAD

In the bead setting, diamonds are set directly into the metal band using very small chisels. Holes are drilled directly into the surface of the metal. A concave depression is made with exact dimensions of each stone to house the gems. This setting was common in the early to middle 20th century and is a lovely choice if you would like something with a more romantic or vintage feel.

HALO

This simply gorgeous setting refers to a placement of diamonds surrounding a center stone like a halo. The halo creates the illusion that the center stone is larger than it is as well as boosting the sparkle and glow of the entire ring. The halo setting is also a very practical way to purchase a smaller carat diamond and still give the effect of a larger stone. A double halo is a series of two rings circling the center stone.

SPLIT SHANK

A split shank is a style featuring a band that separates as it reaches the center setting. Many vintage and antique rings feature this lovely style. The gap created by the split often makes the ring appear larger

and more ornate. A common choice is to embellish the band with a dazzling spread of pavé set diamonds, which help to increase the overall radiant sparkle of the ring.

SOLITAIRE

A solitaire describes one single diamond set beautifully into a ring. Tiffany & Co introduced this setting in 1886 with the first mounted setting of six claws.

ANTIQUE/VINTAGE SETTINGS

Another beautiful and elegant idea for an engagement ring setting is to choose an antique or vintage inspired style. These settings are also known as estate rings. The value of using an antique ring is in the romantic story behind the ring. Perhaps the setting has been passed down from generation to generation. It could also be a newfound treasure that evokes an enchanting new story that infuses your relationship with old world charm. It is possible to purchase a piece of estate jewelry and use a genuine antique ring with a new center stone, or to find a jeweler that has brand new designs that were inspired by vintage rings.

With today's incredible new technological capabilities, a jeweler could easily replicate a stunning vintage setting from a photograph, or use the idea to create a remarkable one-of-a-kind creation. From Edwardian and Victorian to Art Deco or Mid Century designs, the idea of an antique setting is a very lovely choice.

Remember as you choose the setting for your ring to consider not only the beauty but also the durability of the style, as well as how flattering it is for the recipient's hand. Take into consideration lifestyle needs and desires, as well as how comfortable and well crafted the design is, and the value you are getting for the price! Don't forget to consider the ease of daily wear and tear as well as the required care for this setting.

You are making the purchase of a lifetime, so enjoy the process and weigh out all of your exciting options before making your final decision.

MOST POPULAR WEDDING RING STYLES

Channel

Surface

Bead and Bright

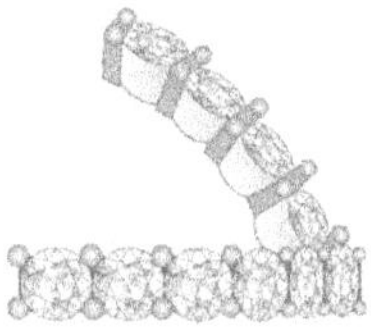

Shared Prong

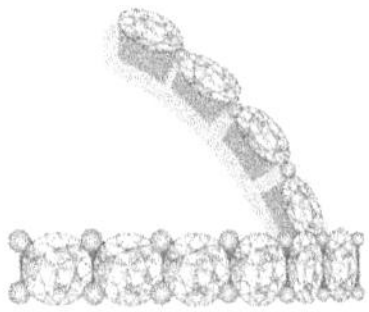

Scallop

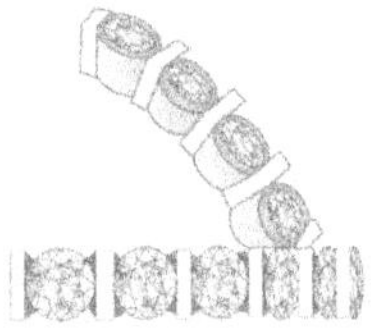

Bar

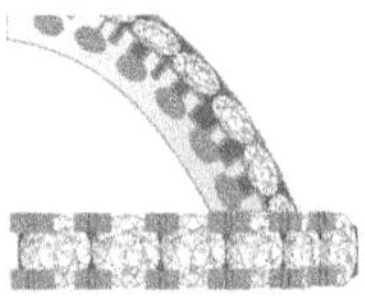

Fishtail

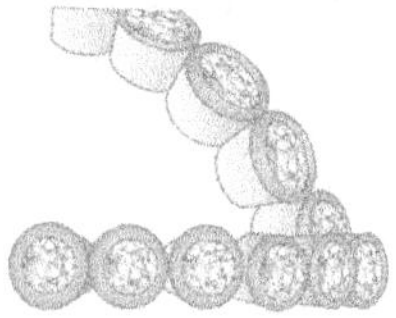

Bezel

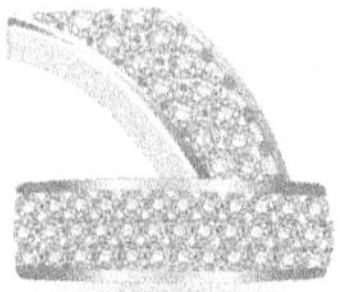

Pavé

Flush

CHAPTER SIX

DESIGN & MANUFACTURING

— OLD VERSUS NEW TECHNIQUES —

CREATING A BEAUTIFUL, finely designed polished diamond ring is an art form that can take many years to master. From labor intensive old world techniques, which rely on expert craftsmanship to hand forge each design, to the exciting technological advancements of 3-D printing, laser & mill machines, as well as Matrix software, there are a variety of methods to produce high quality jewelry today. Discovering how a small object of beauty such as a diamond ring is made is a completely fascinating process that you will learn about in this chapter. To begin, jewelry is manufactured using various techniques. The four methods of fabricating jewelry are: bench made/hand fabricated, die struck/stamping, CAD/casting and 3D printing.

Most pieces of fine jewelry are handmade at some point in the process. A hand-fabricated/bench made ring is not the same thing as a handmade ring, and is considered the highest level of this art form. Hand fabricated rings are the most expensive to purchase. Due to the expertise required to hand fabricate a ring using old world forging techniques, most designer engagement rings available today are generally not made using these labor intensive methods.

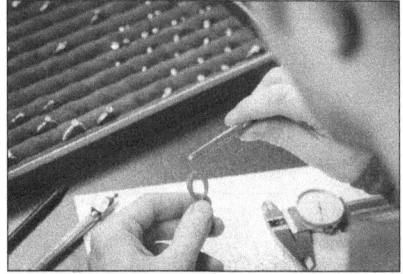

The most common method of manufacturing engagement rings is called casting. The process begins with either a hand carved wax or white metal model, or with a computer generated CAD/CAM model that is then used to make a mold. Molten metal is then poured into the mold to create a rough version of the finished piece. This unique piece is then polished and shaped by hand. The process is a fantastic method to create multiple design ideas.

— STATE OF THE ART TECHNOLOGY —

CAD/CAM & MATRIX SOFTWARE

Matrix Software is computer aided design (CAD/CAM) software to create, analyze, modify and optimize visual designs. It is a state-of-the-art tool that allows professional jewelry designers to create stunning photo realistic three-dimensional (3D) designs on their

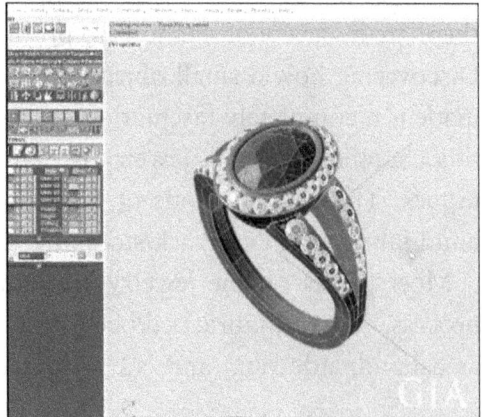

computer screens. The interactive presentations are then output as precise designs used for employing a variety of effective methods including: wax casting, hand-carving and 3D printing technology that bring ideas to life.

CAD/CAM software has been an essential tool in many industries from automobiles to aeronautics to athletic shoes and is now a powerful part of the jewelry making process. This software has transformed the jewelry industry by increasing the level of detail and precision in the modeling process as well as through decreasing the required production time. Models can be designed and saved as well as modified to create many variations on a theme. The possibilities are virtually limitless.

3D PRINTING

The power of modern technology has given rise to an exciting new manufacturing revolution that is a rapidly growing industry. 3D printing is being used in many industries today and is currently becoming widely used for jewelry manufacturing.

3D printing is the process of making three-dimensional products from virtual CAD models. There are multiple methods of 3D printing technology, and what they have in common is that it is an additive process whereby objects are carefully created one

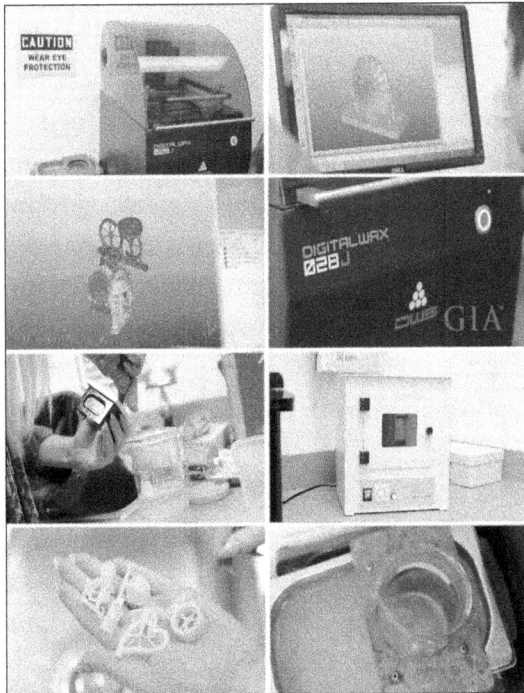

layer at a time. The process is repeated layer by layer till the object is completely printed. In jewelry design, this technique is often used for mold making and casting. Depending on the 3D printing process, it is possible to create pieces directly in metals. Metals that can be 3D printed include brass, cobalt chrome, gold, platinum, silver, stainless steel and titanium. However most jewelry is usually first printed in wax.

The unparalleled accuracy, precision and speed generated by 3D printing technology is quickly transforming the jewelry industry. The benefit of 3D printing is the ability to simplify and speed up the production process, turn ideas into actual three-dimensional objects and significantly reduce manufacturing costs.

LASER MACHINES

From cutting and engraving to welding and repairing, the refined capabilities of laser machines for jewelry production are extraordinary, and have expanded the technical and creative possibilities of jewelry manufacturing exponentially. The intricate details that can be cut in a matter of seconds by these high tech machines are completely astonishing. For a creative designer who might have once been limited by their ability to take an idea and forge it by hand, today the potential for inventive new designs and cutting edge creations is limitless. Laser machines can quickly create perfect, seamless designs, and are easily programmable. This technology is transforming the industry through the level of refinement that can be achieved through these powerful new machines. Designers can now carve and engrave challenging tiny details that would not be possible by hand.

MILL MACHINES

A CNC milling machine or router is larger and heavier than a 3D printer and is considered to be its subtractive equivalent. Though it is a more complex process than 3D printing, milling technology has been around for longer, and therefore the machinery is more evolved.

The process of milling begins with a solid block of material that is then carefully extracted through a cutting process to remove the excess and create intricate shapes that are computer programmed. When it comes to creating very high quality pieces with consistent surface finishes, 3D CNC milling does an excellent job. Though it requires minimal post-production processing, milling is limited to creating only one model at a time and requires a longer set up time than 3D printing where it is possible to produce large batches of similar work at the same time. Mill machines are capable of producing high quality wax models that cast easily, and are perfect for creating master models and custom pieces.

The exciting new technological landscape is providing jewelry designers of today the ability to expand their imagination and create pieces that were once impossible to produce. It is certain that these new technologies will transform the way jewelry is made and open doors for inventive new ideas. By allowing designers to experiment and explore the world of possibilities generated by these new tools, the process of making jewelry is taken to a completely new level.

Uptown Diamond uses state of the art laser machines, 3D printers, polishers and tumblers to create your custom diamond ring.

CHAPTER SEVEN

TIPS FOR BUYING

JUST AS IT IS INVALUABLE to learn all about the details of selecting the right stone, it is critical that you understand the inner workings and industry secrets of the diamond business.

BUYING SHY WITH GREAT PROPORTIONS

A great money-saving strategy is to buy your diamond just under certain key weight thresholds. For example:

- Instead of 2.00 ct you select a 1.89 – 1.99 ct
- Instead of 1.00 ct you select a .90 – .99 ct
- Instead of .50 ct you select a .45 – .49 ct

DIAMOND VALUE

To ensure your diamond keeps its value and continuously appreciates in value buy a diamond that meets the following criteria:

- Natural and untreated
- No Fluorescence
- Clarity Grade SI1 or better (eye clean)
- Color Grade J or better (face up white)
- Cut Grade Class I or II (a well proportioned stone)

SPECIAL LIGHTING

A technique that some jewelry stores will use to make diamonds appear whiter than they actually are is the use of fluorescent lighting to hide nitrogen found in the stones. Consider using a white background when looking at the different color grades of diamonds to see the gem's actual color.

GRADE BUMPING

This is a very sly practice where unethical jewelers take advantage of inexperienced buyers so they can make a greater profit by misrepresenting a diamond's color and/or clarity grade. Since it is rather difficult for an untrained eye to classify a diamond's exact properties, a buyer can easily be put into a disadvantageous position by a dishonest jeweler. Unfortunately, technicalities in the Federal Trade Commission's regulation make this unscrupulous widespread phenomenon completely legal. The regulations state that a diamond can legally be sold within one color and one clarity grade of the original stone's classification. That is why it is imperative to buy a bonded diamond.

DEPOSITS

Under certain circumstances it is commonplace for jewelers to require a deposit that would end up locking you into purchasing only from them. The following are situations that you should be aware of:

Example 1: You want to have an independent appraisal of the diamond

Under this scenario you might be obligated to pay in full for the diamond as a form of insurance for the jeweler. This might seem completely legitimate, until you return with an unacceptable report from an appraiser showing that the stone was misrepresented. Realizing this, you have decided you don't want to purchase that diamond, but the jeweler only allows you to receive a refund in the form of a matching store credit locking you into purchasing from a jeweler whom you do not feel comfortable.

Example 2: You are interested in viewing a diamond that is not a part of the jeweler's inventory and it will require shipping and insurance fees to transport the stone to their site.

Provided you like the stone, these fees could be integrated into the final ring purchase. If, however, you are unhappy with the stone and decide you do not want to purchase it, you should only be required to pay for the transportation and insurance fees related to viewing this stone. I recommend walking away from the situation if the jeweler asks you for a deposit larger than the shipping/insurance fees.

SET & STICK TO YOUR BUDGET

By creating a predetermined budget before shopping for your diamond, you can keep yourself focused only on what is available within your price range and ignore everything else that will tempt you. This will prevent you from being coaxed into spending more money and making a purchase you might later regret. Watch out for *opportunities* and *deals* that ultimately are just too good to be true. Why would a jeweler want to sell a product below market value? Considering that diamonds are one of the most in demand commodities on the planet, high quality diamonds are rarely sold at a discount!

LAB REPORTS & HOW TO READ THEM

If you want to be absolutely certain that your diamond is exactly what has been described by the jeweler, invest in an official lab report from a reputable gemological laboratory such as GIA. It is important to remember that just because a diamond has a lab grading report, it does not mean it is a great diamond. Great diamonds can have lab grading reports and poor diamonds can also have lab grading reports. Below you will find a sample report from the GIA as well as a guide on how to read them.

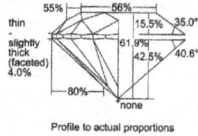

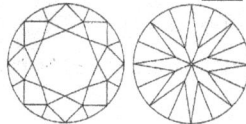

1 | Header: Who Graded the Diamond?

In this area you will identify the lab issuing this report. Though there are many labs that provide this service, it is well known that the GIA has strict, dependable and unbiased grading standards that consumers can trust.

2 | Report Number, Shape/Cutting Style & Measurements

Report Number: In this section you will find the report number, which will be valuable should you ever lose the document and need your lab to reissue one. In most circumstances this number would also be used for online verification.

Cutting Style: The next line describes the stone's shape and cutting style. (Such as *round brilliant*)

Measurements: This line defines the stone's physical dimensions in millimeters.

3 | Grading Results: The Four Cs

Carat Weight: This field defines the weight of the stone measured to the hundredth of a carat.

Color Grade: This grade determines the lack of color within a diamond.

Clarity Grade: Examined under a 10X microscope loupe to determine inclusions, imperfections/blemishes

Cut Grade: This grading is based on a scale of excellent to poor.

4 | Additional Grading Information

Polish: This defines the smoothness of the diamond's polished surface.

Symmetry: This field refers to the relationship between the polished facets of the finished stone.

Fluorescence: This describes the level at which the stone glows under an Ultraviolet (UV) light.

5   Diagrams

Here you will find visual representations of the unique characteristics of the diamond, including symbols outlining the specific locations of the stone's markings. External *blemishes* are marked in the color green on the document, while internal *inclusions* are marked in red. The proportions diagram defines in percentages the following attributes: table, depth, crown angles, pavilion depth, pavilion angle, girdle and culet.

6   Security Features & Authenticity Marks

These features are usually found in the form of a hologram, a UPC code or embossed stamp, and prove the authenticity of the document. Additionally, most labs provide an online service so you can quickly verify the legitimacy of your document.

WARRANTIES AND GUARANTEES

When shopping for your diamond, expect to encounter a variety of different offers regarding warranties and guarantees. You are making a sizable investment, and as a consumer it is important for you to consider the best way for you to protect your asset. Be aware that if you are required to pay for a warranty or guarantee, immediately consider this a red flag. You shouldn't have to pay for a warranty or a guarantee! Many businesses will play games with you by charging a fee for their warranties. If the diamond is worth what the dealer is selling it for, then they should back the diamond 100%. It is important that as a customer, you feel completely confident in what you are purchasing and the amount you are spending for that product and/ or service. Always read the fine print! Remember, a diamond with a good guarantee will always protect you as a consumer because if for any reason you don't think your purchase was a good deal, you will be able to return it.

On the next page you will find the most common offers that you will see in the current market:

30 Day Guarantee: This is by far the most common offer you will see. After making your purchase, you have 30 days to return for a full refund, no questions asked. Unfortunately, after just 30 short days, you will be stuck with your purchase. An uneducated consumer might not realize after the excitement of the purchase the actual quality of the diamond isn't what they thought it was, find themselves disappointed and unable to make a change.

90 Day Guarantee: With this guarantee, obviously you would have a little more room to decide, but you still only have 90 days to consider whether the ring is or is not perfect for you.

NO Guarantee: Think twice about purchasing a diamond without a guarantee! What would happen if your plans don't work out, or you don't get engaged?! It's like playing Russian Roulette, and that is just not worth the headache. No matter how good of a deal you think you are getting, if there is no guarantee just walk away.

Double to Get Anything: This is a sneaky situation where the customer purchases a $10,000 engagement ring and decides a year later that they want to upgrade and exchange it for a $12,000 ring, but the jeweler offers the customer credit for the $10,000 purchase ONLY if they spend double the original purchase price ($20,000) thereby forcing you into a bigger ticket item. Again, read the fine print!

Lifetime Guarantee: The philosophy at **Uptown Diamond** is that we provide exceptional service and the best quality products and that we are willing to backup for a lifetime. We offer a lifetime guarantee on the center stones of our engagement rings so our clients can feel 100% confident in their purchase.

Ask for Paperwork: Most of the paperwork you receive from a jeweler will state that **it is not** a guarantee, valuation and/or appraisal. Protect yourself by making certain they give you a document that is a legitimate guarantee, valuation and/or appraisal so you can hold the jeweler liable for your purchase.

— MY DIAMOND CHECKLIST —

These are seven essential questions to ask yourself before setting out to find a jeweler and begin the search for your perfect diamond:

1. What is my budget?

2. What shape diamond is preferred?

3. What carat size am I looking for?

4. What type of metal do I want for my setting?

5. What type of setting is ideal for my diamond?

6. What finger size ring do I need?

7. What is my time frame?

QUESTIONS TO ASK — PROSPECTIVE JEWELERS —

Take into consideration what matters to you most as you search for your jeweler, from personal attention and professionalism to their willingness to educate you and provide you with top quality customer service. Notice when you speak to the salesperson if they answer your questions or if they avoid them. Are they transparent or do you feel like they are being deceptive?

The following is a list of important questions to help you find a great jeweler to work with so you can purchase the perfect diamond. A good strategy would be to call a few local jewelers and have them answer these questions. When you find two or three who get the highest rating, make an appointment to meet them in person. The odds will be in your favor if you get a great answer to all of these questions.

— PROSPECTIVE JEWELER QUESTIONNAIRE —

1. Do you specialize in diamonds?

2. Are your diamonds loose (unmounted) diamonds?

3. How large is your inventory of loose diamonds?

4. Do you custom cut diamonds?

5. Are your stones bonded?

6. How do your prices compare to wholesale prices?

7. Do you craft your own jewelry on-site?

8. Where are you located?

9. How long have you been in business?

10. What is the history of this company?

11. Do you see customers by appointment or walk-in?

12. Are you an American Gem Society (AGS) rated jeweler?

13. Is there a GIA Gemologist on staff?

14. Do you supply a diamond lab grading report?

15. Do you have a viewing laboratory for gems?

16. Do you have a master set of diamonds for color grading?

17. Do you have a UV light to check for fluorescence?

18. Do you have a 10x – 20.5mm triplet loupe?

19. Do you have a gem scope or microscope for viewing?

20. Do you provide a Sarin or Megascope Report?

21. Do you have an electronic scale to weigh diamonds?

22. What is your return policy?

23. What is your buy back policy?

24. What guarantees do you have?

25. Do you manufacture on-site?

26. Do you have an on-site graphic designer?

27. Do you do 3D wax mockups?

28. How long does the process take from start to finish?

29. Do you have financing?

30. How could I get financing?

31. Can I pay with a credit card?

32. How do I insure my diamond?

33. Do you take care/maintain the diamond?

34. If something happens to my ring will you help me fix it? Do you repair jewelry and how skilled are you?

Before you decide to invest your precious time and money in developing a relationship with a prospective jeweler, it is helpful for you to be 100% clear about your interaction. The following list of ten questions will help you decide how to proceed and clarify if this is the right choice for you.

ASK YOURSELF THE — FOLLOWING QUESTIONS —

1. Do you feel heard by the jeweler? Do they listen respectfully to you?

2. Does the staff seem trustworthy, knowledgeable and do they answer your questions with ease?

3. Is this a business that will be around in 10 years? 20 years? Will they be around if you need repairs?

4. Can they create custom pieces? Do they do the work themselves or outsource?

5. Are they willing to go the extra mile and help you find something you will really love?

6. Do you feel respected and appreciated by them, or are they just after another sale?

7. Do you feel safe trusting them with your precious gemstones?

8. Do they treat your jewelry with respect?

9. Are they nice people? Does it feel pleasant to work with them?

CHAPTER EIGHT

AFTER THE PURCHASE

— CARING FOR YOUR DIAMOND —

YOU ADORE YOUR precious ring and want to ensure that it is in perfect condition on a regular basis. It will surprise you how much the slightest amount of dirt can reduce the sparkle of your diamond.

Just because a diamond is one of the world's hardest substances, doesn't mean it can't chip or scratch. Protect your ring while doing daily chores such as cleaning your home or working on any kind of project that uses your hands extensively. If you are going out, and plan to work with your hands or do any kind of major physical activity, consider leaving your ring at home.

Aside from chips and scratches, many chemicals including daily household cleaning products such as bleach can damage or dull your ring.

We all know the old saying *better safe than sorry*. When it comes to your diamond ring, you will be much happier in the long run if you proceed with caution. The following are a few professional tips to help you take care of your ring and ensure that it stays radiant for years to come:

DAILY HANDLING

Always pick up a gemstone ring by the metal band. This will help ensure the strength of your diamond's setting and increase the longevity of its security.

Everything from hand soap and body lotions to hair spray, powders, makeup and the natural oils from your fingers can create a film of grease that negatively alters the way your diamond looks. For this reason, be aware of how you handle your ring so it can stay luminescent.

Though it might seem obvious, DON'T remove your ring in public! Many people have washed their hands in a public facility and either forgotten their ring or accidentally dropped it down the drain!

WHEN TO TAKE OFF YOUR RING

- Housecleaning
- Playing sports
- Gardening
- Swimming in the pool or ocean
- Cooking
- Putting on lotions, cosmetics or perfume

HOW TO CLEAN YOUR RING

Regular cleanings will keep your jewelry in top condition. For rings worn on a daily basis, we recommend cleaning them once a week. Here's a simple and effective method using everyday household products to keep your diamond jewelry looking radiant:

What you will need:

- 3 small glass bowls
- ¼ cup of ammonia
- dishwashing liquid
- warm water
- toothbrush
- rubber gloves
- paper towel or soft towel

1. **SOAK:** Gently place your ring in a glass bowl filled with 1 cup of warm water and ¼ cup of ammonia. Let the ring soak for twenty minutes. This will help remove dirt that has built up in the setting of your ring.

2. **WASH:** Put on some rubber gloves to protect yourself from the potency of your cleaning solution. Remove the ring from the solution and place it in the second glass bowl filled with a solution of warm water and a little dishwashing liquid. Gently move the ring around in the solution.

3. **SCRUB:** Using a toothbrush, begin to scrub your ring. Brush across the stone and into the setting of the ring working your way across all the crevices of your ring.

4. **RINSE:** Remove the ring from the soapy solution and rinse it in the third bowl filled with warm water. Make sure to remove all of the soap. Place the ring gently on a soft cloth or paper towel to absorb the excess water. Allow it to dry completely and you are ready to shine!

A common method of cleaning jewelry is with an ultrasonic cleaner that uses high frequency sound waves through a detergent solution to effectively remove stubborn dirt.

Please note that fragile settings and estate jewelry are best cleaned by a professional jeweler. Never use commercial cleaners or solutions made with ammonia on pearls.

It can be problematic for some gemstones, so be cautious. A newer, effective method that is safe for all gemstones is the ionic cleaner.

MAINTENANCE

Just like you schedule visits to see the doctor or get your oil checked for your car, schedule check-ups with your jeweler! It's important to make sure that your gem is secure in its setting and in perfect condition. We recommend visiting your jeweler every six months to a year (depending on how hard you are on your ring) to inspect your setting and have your ring professionally cleaned. Many jewelers will provide this service for their clients free of charge.

STORAGE

Diamonds are capable of scratching other jewelry, so the best way to store them is in their own beautiful soft fabric lined pouch or in a separate jewelry box that protects them from any kind of damage. In addition to safeguarding your ring from scratches, consider storing your valuable jewelry in a secure and hidden place.

TRAVEL

In the event that you plan to travel somewhere that wearing your ring could make you a target for muggers or thieves, just leave your precious jewels safe at home.

Though you might love wearing your ring everywhere you go and feel attached to its symbolism and importance, sometimes it's just wiser to detract attention from yourself. Some neighborhoods and countries are filled with people who are suffering and impoverished, and you would just be better off if they didn't notice you at all. If you happen to find yourself in this kind of uncomfortable situation and are wearing your ring, turn the stone into the center of your palm so only the band shows on the outside.

If you choose to take valuable jewelry with you when traveling, always keep it with you. Never leave it in a checked bag or easily accessible in your hotel room. Be aware that the mini safe found in hotel rooms can easily be opened by a professional thief. Hotels often provide safety deposit boxes at the front desk. If you are traveling abroad with valuable jewelry, it is also a good idea to have a photograph of your jewelry printed, dated and notarized beforehand, proving that you did not purchase it overseas. This will protect you from being forced to pay a hefty customs fee.

— PROTECT YOUR INVESTMENT —

INSURANCE & APPRAISAL

Life is always full of surprises and for that reason it's important to protect your assets. No matter how cautious you are, there is always the chance of your ring getting lost or being stolen.

Even though your ring is truly irreplaceable, insuring your diamond ring will provide you with a sense of security knowing that under the worst circumstances your investment is covered. In the event that something unwanted occurs, your insurance will reimburse you for the value of the ring.

Some homeowners or renters insurance policies will offer an extension (or rider) that covers diamond rings, so ask your company for specific details about what they offer. Usually they will only cover your valuables up to a certain dollar amount. If you want more coverage, insure your ring with a company that specializes in insuring jewelry. Most diamond jewelry insurance policies will require that you get an independent appraisal to determine the value of your ring. We recommend having your ring appraised right after you receive it.

While many jewelers will offer an on-site appraisal, finding an independent, non-biased appraiser who can give you an outside opinion is very important. If you aren't sure where to find one, contact The American Gem Society (AGS) and they will guide you. Seek a reputable, independent appraiser with top gemological and appraisal credentials who is a member of a national appraisal society. You can also hire an appraiser before purchasing a ring to assist you in the process and help you make a more educated decision.

For insurance purposes, it is a good idea to get a new appraisal every three to five years. Your investment will most likely increase, and you will want to make sure that your appraisal papers are up to date in order to protect yourself in the case of loss.

An Expert's Opinion
TO INSURE OR NOT TO INSURE
WRITTEN BY J. MACE MEEKS, PRINCIPAL OF INSGROUP, INC

Throughout your life, you will probably question whether or not you should invest in insurance … wondering to yourself— should I hedge my bet and pay the premium to protect my asset or roll the dice and go *blind nello* with no insurance coverage and save the premium dollars?

When you purchase your first piece of fine jewelry, whether it is an engagement ring or a fine watch, you have a decision to make— *To Insure or Not to Insure?* You are essentially left with those two questions once you have purchased that beautiful diamond ring… actually you are left with three different options if you choose to insure your investment (that is exactly what a quality diamond or a fine piece of jewelry is… an investment).

As I begin to detail the three options on how to insure your jewelry, I will briefly touch on the fourth option—no insurance (otherwise known as *blind nello*). There are two reasons why you shouldn't insure a fine piece of jewelry.

1. You are wealthy enough to immediately replace your purchase when it is lost, stolen or damaged.

2. It is a fake.

If you do not fall under the *wealthy* category (or if you do and you want to hedge your potential loss) and you choose to protect your beautiful jewelry by purchasing insurance to cover your investment, I will detail the three most common ways to insure.

OPTION ONE: SCHEDULING OF JEWELRY

This is the most common and preferred form of protecting your jewelry. It is usually insured as part of your homeowner's (or renter's) insurance policy by scheduling the actual piece of jewelry. *Scheduling* in simple terms means to list the actual piece of jewelry with the exact description of the item and the value or amount of insurance you would like placed on the item. For example, 2 carat diamond engagement ring: platinum, with 2 carat G clarity flawless diamond – $50,000.00.

The above example is predicated as an appraisal given by a certified (keyword) gemologist to justify the value to the insurance carrier. This is the only way an insurance carrier will schedule an item for an appraised amount. To schedule a piece of jewelry is the safest way to protect your investment for the appraised amount. If the item is stolen, damaged or mysteriously disappears the insurance carrier will cover the item for the appraised value.

Having a certified appraisal from your jeweler is the only way this happens. The cost of this varies by insurance carrier and by value of the item, but should average between $1.50 to $2.00 per $100 of coverage ($20,000 item = $20,000 ÷ 100 = 200 x $1.70 = $340.00 annual premium).

OPTION TWO: BLANKET COVERAGE

Having the option to insure your jewelry under the form of blanket coverage is usually up to the actual insurance carrier you are insured with, not all carriers allow this. Blanket coverage allows you to set parameters on the actual value per item and the aggregate amount of total coverage. I would recommend using this form of coverage along with scheduling your most valued items of jewelry.

An example of blanket coverage would be to have $10,000 maximum coverage per item with an aggregate amount of coverage up to $50,000. You would have coverage for all items with a value of $10,000 or less up to a total value of $50,000 paid. This is a great way to insure the majority of your jewelry without having to schedule every item you may own.

As I mentioned earlier, having your most valued items scheduled and your other items covered under a blanket amount is a great combination of coverage and usually not as costly from a premium standpoint.

OPTION THREE: USING JEWELRY COVERAGE INCLUDED UNDER YOUR HOMEOWNERS/RENTERS POLICY

Most homeowners insurance policies (or renters policy) have a jewelry endorsement added to the policy that covers stated amount of jewelry coverage. This is not the form of coverage you want to rely on to cover your prized possession(s). This endorsement is only designed to cover a specific amount of coverage, usually from $500 to $10,000 in total coverage. It also states that a loss is only covered if there is forced entry to your home, condo or apartment and the loss is subject to some form of deductible (no coverage available unless loss is over a certain amount). The deductible is usually the same as your homeowner's or renter's deductible and could be quite high. There is a reason this type of coverage is usually thrown in for minimal premium...it is hardly ever used due to the forced entry language and high deductible. I would never recommend this to be your only form of jewelry coverage if you own several valued pieces of jewelry.

They say, "you sometimes get what you pay for..." and in the case of insuring your jewelry items, that is a fact. Always consult your insurance agent as to what coverage meets your specific needs and ask all the questions you need answered to feel like you have designed a tailor made insurance program specific to your needs. Insurance coverage should be designed, just like your jewelry, to fit you and only you.

CHAPTER NINE

WEDDING TRADITIONS

FOR THOUSANDS OF YEARS, every facet of a wedding, from the engagement to the honeymoon, has been richly steeped in cultural traditions, religious beliefs and ancestral superstitions. These cherished customs have been infused into our modern day society and many of us are still unaware of the meaning behind the old world wedding traditions.

Many popular wedding rituals are rooted in old European and Egyptian customs. These ancient traditions were once new ideas that have thrived by being passed down from generation to generation. As gender equality has gained momentum, many of these old traditions are going out of style, and wedding etiquette is changing today. When you sit down to plan your wedding, reflect upon what old customs you want to continue that are meaningful to you, and consider cultivating exciting new traditions that express the individuality and creativity of your new family.

Have you ever wondered why the bride wears a garter belt or tosses the wedding bouquet over her head? What is the actual meaning behind the old tradition of *something old, something new, something borrowed, something blue?* Why can't the groom see his bride-to-be before the wedding? Why does he carry his bride over the threshold? What's the idea behind breaking a glass? We have included some of the more popular wedding traditions for your enjoyment.

THE VEIL: This ancient tradition has a variety of meanings depending on religion and culture, as veils have had great symbolism throughout history. It is believed that the veil predates the wedding dress by four centuries. Dating as far back to the Crusades, women were bargained for and given away by their father. On the wedding day, a man would finally meet his wife, right after the marriage ceremony! The bride would be hidden behind a veil, only to be seen by her husband after

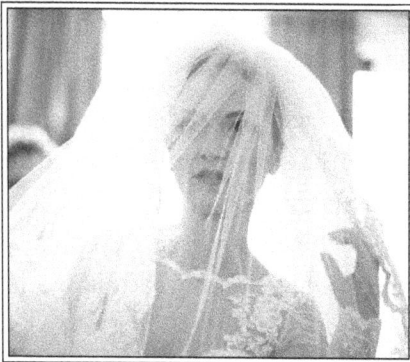

the wedding. This has also been a tradition in some Middle Eastern and Asian cultures, where marriages were arranged. In Rome, Italy, a bride would wear a veil down the wedding aisle in order to protect herself from evil spirits who were envious of her happiness. Veils are also seen as a symbol of purity, innocence and chasteness in many cultures, as well as to represent that love and beauty are not only skin deep. In the Jewish tradition, it is believed that the feminine aspect of the divine shines through the bride's face. The veil symbolizes a sense of privacy between the radiance of the holiness of the feminine aspect and her connection with the divine spirit. The belief is that as the bride and groom are about to marry and become one, her sacred radiance remains hidden from the world, and can only be revealed to her husband. The lifting of the veil has been seen as a significant part of the wedding ceremony, as either the father revealing the bride to the new husband or the groom lifting the veil, as a symbol of the groom receiving his new bride, or in some cultures taking her as his possession.

SOMETHING OLD, NEW, BORROWED and BLUE: This superstition dates back to an old English rhyme recited in the Victorian era that read:

> *"Something old, something new,*
> *Something borrowed, something blue,*
> *And a silver sixpence in her shoe."*

The bride-to-be was instructed to gather these five objects in order to have good luck on her wedding day: something old symbolizes tradition and continuity, something new represents hope and a bright new future. Something borrowed is usually from a happily married family member or friend and refers to transferring good luck and happiness to the new bride. In the Christian tradition, blue has been associated with weddings and purity as the Virgin Mary wore a blue dress. It also references fidelity and love. The British custom of wearing a sixpence in your shoe refers to wealth and prosperity, but this tradition is not part of American wedding rituals.

RAIN ON YOUR WEDDING DAY: Some people believe rain on your wedding day is good luck, while some believe it is bad luck! Here are some beliefs why rain brings good luck on your wedding day:

- In agricultural societies rain symbolizes fertility and growth and having children.
- It represents the last tears a bride will finally shed in her life over love.
- Rain washes and cleans away old memories and brings a fresh new start.

SEEING THE BRIDE BEFORE THE WEDDING: During unromantic times when families arranged their children's marriage, and the wedding was partially a business transaction between two families in order to gain wealth for the bride's family, it was forbidden to see the bride before the wedding ceremony. This was a way to prevent the groom from changing his mind and shaming the potential bride's family, especially if he was not attracted to his bride-to-be and wanted to call off the wedding. In today's modern society many couples still follow this tradition, though times are changing. Around the world, and in many religious traditions and cultures, the betrothed couple meet before the wedding ceremony to partake in rituals such as signing the ketubah in the Jewish tradition, tea ceremonies in Asian cultures and other sacred marriage rituals. A new way that couples today are considering this option is as a part of the magic of this extraordinary emotionally charged occasion in their lives, and reveling in the moment of seeing each other for the *first time*.

GIVING AWAY THE BRIDE: The meaning of the word wedding is actually derived from the meaning *to gamble* or *to wage*. This ancient custom also dates back to the days when women were seen as their father's property until they were wagered and *given away* for a dowry only to become property of their husband. Thankfully, times have changed and *most* cultures no longer view women in this way. This age old tradition is still a beautiful way for parents to show their love and appreciation as well as to give blessings to the new couple. Many modern couples are finding appropriate new ways to breathe life into this old custom and make it their own.

THE KISS: The symbolism of the kiss goes beyond affection at a wedding. The kiss is what seals the deal. It is also seen as an exchange of souls as the couple transmits their essence into their partner, to unite as one and be eternally bonded together.

THE WEDDING RING: Throughout history, the ring has been seen as a powerful symbol both of eternal love, as well as a symbol of ownership. In ancient Egypt, the circle represented eternity, and an unending bond, while the emptiness in the center signified the entryway into the mystery of the unknown. The wedding ring has been worn on different fingers and different hands depending on the culture. Jewelry throughout the ages has been seen as a symbol of bonding. Early rings were made out of hemp, leather bone or ivory. In Ancient Roman culture, they believed there was a vein called *vena amoris (the vein of love)* that ran from the fourth finger of the left hand, directly to the heart.

THROWING RICE: Since early Roman times grains such as wheat and rice have been associated with fertility and prosperity. After the couple was married, their guests would throw wheat or rice at the couple to transmit blessings to the bride and groom. The rice and grains were believed to ward off evil spirits, wish them good luck and grant them fertility. Some cultures made offerings of rice to the gods as a prayer of protection for the newlyweds.

THROWING CONFETTI: This Italian born tradition follows suit with the tradition of throwing rice at the new couple, and the word confetti is actually derived from *confetto* which are delicious sugar coated almonds that are given as part of traditional Italian gifts at weddings, birthdays and communions that also symbolize good fortune and prosperity. Paper confetti has become a popular wedding tradition in many cultures and it looks vibrantly festive in photographs. If you decide to use confetti at your wedding, make sure to use a kind of paper that won't stain anyone's clothing (especially the bride's gown). Other popular fun modern alternatives to confetti and rice include: bubbles, rose petals or other soft flower petals, balloons, sparklers, butterflies or streamers. Another Italian tradition is to release a duo of doves, representing the couple and signifying love and happiness.

CARRYING THE BRIDE OVER THE THRESHOLD: In many parts of the world this ancient tradition started by the Romans still prevails. The bride is carried by the groom till she is taken over the threshold of her new home. This is to protect her from bad luck or demons that might inhabit the home and enter her body through the soles of her feet. Today this tradition has transformed and is seen more as something chivalrous and joyful!

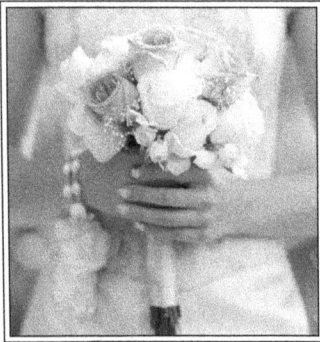

THE BRIDAL BOUQUET: Flowers have always held great meaning and the appreciation of flowers continues to evolve through time. Early bridal bouquets consisted of garlic and aromatic pungent herbs, which were believed to contain mystical powers to ward evil spirits away from the bride on her wedding day and bring her good luck. These bouquets also symbolized fertility and devotion, growth and renewal. Around the 1700s, women started to carry beautiful bouquets of flowers in place of herbs to bring elegance, grace, scent and color to their wedding day. Flower experts who understand *florigraphy—the language of flowers*, explain that each flower carries its own symbolism and meaning. Cultures around the world believe different flowers hold sacred meanings for wedding ceremonies.

THE BRIDAL GARTER and THE BOUQUET TOSS: In 14th century France, it was believed that owning a piece of a bride's wedding dress would bring the guests good fortune. The guests would literally tear pieces of the bride's dress off of her in hopes of becoming the next to marry. To preserve their beautiful dresses, brides started throwing other articles of clothing such as the bouquet and the garter to the guests. In Medieval times, the garter symbolized the groom relinquishing the virginal status of his new bride. He threw the garter at his male guests to distract them and keep them away from his new bride.

BREAKING GLASS: At the end of a Jewish wedding ceremony, the groom customarily steps on a glass and breaks it as a symbol of the binding nature of the wedded relationship. The glass is broken to remind the couple that relationships are fragile and must be taken care of or they will break. As the newlyweds stand together on their wedding day, experiencing a heightened moment of happiness, the glass is broken to remind them that life is full of both sadness and joy, and that they must support each other through both.

RINGING BELLS: Like many of the other superstitious wedding traditions, the symbolism of this Irish tradition was intended to ward off evil spirits and to bring good fortune to the new couple. In rural areas, bells would ring across the countryside to spread the church's news across the land. Though most people today don't focus on warding off evil spirits, bells are often seen as a symbol of unity, love, joy and a new beginning.

— SPECIAL OCCASIONS —

Throughout history, diamonds have held great meaning and power. Known because of its impermeable strength as *The Stone of Invincibility*, the diamond has been heralded for centuries as a magnificent gem that symbolizes affluence, love, fidelity, strength, purity, power and perfection. Written about in many ancient culture's lore, the king of all stones has been said to increase the love of a husband for his wife, and is legendary for the infinite power it grants to its wearer.

From Marilyn Monroe to Moulin Rouge, women have been glamorously singing about their love of diamonds for years. While most people associate diamond rings with engagements and weddings, they make fantastic gifts for many other special occasions.

Nothing can compare to the exhilarating feeling of receiving a luxurious and thoughtful gift of a carefully curated diamond ring, necklace, pendant, bracelet or earrings. Every time your loved one puts on that beautiful piece of jewelry, they will remember the time it was given to them and cherish this deeply personal gift for life.

Momentous occasions such as anniversaries and birthdays, pregnancy, childbirth and graduation are some of the perfect opportunities to give jewelry as a gift. Consider heightening the romance of Valentine's Day, or memorializing Mother's or Father's Day with a stunning diamond. Nothing sparkles brighter in the winter air than a glittering diamond for Christmas or Chanukah.

Special days or milestones that are of significant importance to your loved ones can become unforgettable occasions that you can make even more memorable by honoring them with the gift of a lovely piece of jewelry. Pay tribute to remarkable experiences and places that bond you together, as well as extraordinary moments that you want to preserve.

Honor a significant occasion for life, with the power of words or symbols, by engraving the jewelry with a personalized message or mark that holds a uniquely private story. The gift of fine jewelry is a meaningful symbol of your love and appreciation that will be treasured for life.

Wedding anniversaries are a special time for married couples to honor and reflect on the love that they share together. Throughout the world there are various ways to celebrate wedding anniversaries. The desire to memorialize special moments and significant dates filled with personal meaning is something that has been an integral part of Western culture for many centuries.

Traditional anniversary celebrations include each spouse giving gifts to one another as a way of commemorating the years shared together, as well as to symbolize a milestone in their marriage. The gifts in the early years are intended to be practical and useful as the couple begins to build a home together. Additionally, each year's gift holds deep significance in its meaning for the married couple. For example, the traditional first wedding anniversary gift is paper, and it symbolizes the power and strength of the interwoven fibers. The modern tradition of watches or clocks for the first anniversary represents eternal love that extends beyond time.

ANNIVERSARY GIFT LIST

Years 1 - 70	Traditional Gifts	Modern Gifts	Gemstones
1st	Paper	Clocks, Watches	Gold
2nd	Cotton	China	Garnet
3rd	Leather	Crystal, Glass	Pearls
4th	Flowers, Fruits	Linen, Appliances	Blue Topaz
5th	Wood	Silverware	Sapphire
6th	Iron, Candy	Wood	Amethyst
7th	Wool, Copper, Brass	Table Sets	Onyx
8th	Bronze	Linen, Lace	Tourmaline
9th	Pottery, Willow	Leather	Lapis
10th	Tin, Aluminum, Pewter	Diamonds	Diamond
11th	Steel	Fashion Jewelry	Turquoise
12th	Silk	Pearls, Gems	Jade
13th	Lace	Textiles	Citrine, Moonstone
14th	Ivory	Gold Jewelry	Opal, Agate
15th	Crystal	Watches	Ruby, Crystal
16th	Topaz	Hollowware	Peridot, Aquamarine
17th	Amethyst, Citrine	Furniture	Amethyst, Citrine
18th	Garnet	Porcelain	Cat's Eye
19th	Aquamarine	Bronze	Garnet
20th	China, Porcelain	Platinum	Emerald
25th	Silver	Silver Jewelry	Silver Jubilee
30th	Pearl	Diamond	Pearl Jubilee
35th	Coral	Jade	Emerald
40th	Ruby	Ruby	Ruby
45th	Sapphire	Sapphire	Sapphire
50th	Gold	Gold	Golden Jubilee
55th	Emerald	Turquoise	Alexandrite
60th	Diamond	Gold	Diamond Jubilee
70th	Platinum	Iron	Smokey Quartz

— A BRIEF HISTORY OF BIRTHSTONES —

A Roman-Jewish 1st Century Historian named Josephus tells us that birthstones were first represented in the breastplate of Aaron that had stones for each of the twelve months in the year or the 12 signs of the zodiac. In later centuries it was written that the 12 stones lined up with the 12 apostles. It was even believed in more modern times, folklore that wearing any of the birthstones during its corresponding month would enhance therapeutic properties. It wasn't until 1912 that the National Association of Jewelers made a standard list which was updated in 1952 by the Jewelry Industry Council of America. Additional stones have been added to the months and a few replacements have been made through the years based on style and availability.

BIRTHSTONE CHART	
January	Garnet
February	Amethyst
March	Aquamarine
April	Diamond
May	Emerald
June	Pearl
July	Ruby
August	Peridot
September	Sapphire
October	Opal
November	Topaz
December	Turquoise

CHAPTER TEN

PROSALS

The following are some proposals of a few of Uptown Diamond's clients. It was our pleasure to be part of these special moments.

ROMAN HOLIDAY
Rob & Jaclyn

The Ring Process: When I decided that I was going to propose to my girlfriend Jaclyn, I knew that I didn't want to go to a jewelry chain in the mall but preferred to have a custom ring made especially for her. Not knowing where to start, I went online and searched on Google, which led me to reading Yelp reviews about Uptown Diamond. Inspired by all of the positive reviews, I decided to stop in one day to meet Rick Antona. I was expecting his office to be a jewelry store, not a private office in the bottom of a professional building, so I hadn't made a prior appointment.

As soon as I walked in the door, the receptionist was very friendly and immediately called the back office to see if Rick could meet with me. Within just a few seconds he was in the lobby walking me back to his office (which by the way is AMAZING! The walls are covered in memorabilia from his athletic championship ring designs.)

We sat down and I showed him pictures of what I wanted to design. He told me it wouldn't be a problem and just to email him the pictures. We spoke about the diamonds that would wrap around the band and instead of him trying to upsell me on them, Rick told me exactly the size and clarity I SHOULD get so the look wouldn't diminish the look of the center stone. After we decided on this part and the metal for the band, Rick told me that he would have his graphic designer come up with artwork for the ring and email the pictures to me. The next step would be to approve the artwork, and then he would print out a 3D mold of the ring, so we could place the center stone and approve the ring design before the actual manufacturing process.

What an easy and painless process! I visited the office three times. The first time to meet him. The second time to approve the 3D model and the third time to pick up the finished ring. Rick Antona is a super nice guy and I could not have asked for a better experience! I've actually sent a couple of friends to him. Highly recommend!

The Proposal: Thanks to Rick and his team at Uptown Diamond I had the perfect, custom, one of a kind ring to ask Jaclyn to be my wife. The next step was figuring out exactly where and how. I wanted the proposal to be something she would remember forever and a story to share with her friends and family.

Rick asked me how I was planning on proposing and at that moment I wasn't sure. We had a trip planned to visit Italy with a group of friends in the coming month, and I asked him what he thought about proposing to her then. We both agreed that it was the perfect time to propose since it was a group trip, and she wouldn't expect it.

The trip included travelling to Rome, Florence and Venice. Everyone I spoke to said that out of the three locations Rome was the least romantic place to propose. The places I found that might have been good locations were under construction. However, after speaking with my friends, we agreed it would be better to propose in Rome so that the rest of the trip could be an engagement party! I carried the ring carefully in my jacket pocket the entire time waiting for the perfect moment. Everyone but Jaclyn knew what was going on. During our second day in Rome we took a guided tour of the Colosseum followed by Palatine Hill. I thought the Colosseum could be a great place, but realized it was overcrowded with tourists. Then we began our tour of Palatine Hill. Jaclyn and I split off from the tour with another couple we were traveling with. The girls saw this amazing tree where they wanted to have their picture taken. They handed us the cameras and took off for the tree. My buddy leaned over and said, "This might be the spot." I already knew it was.

Jaclyn loves taking pictures of nature and we were finally by ourselves. There was nobody else around. After we took the girls' picture together, I said that I wanted to take one with Jaclyn. When we got to the tree, I told Jaclyn how much I loved her and how happy I was to be there with her. I told her that there is nobody that I love more in the world and no one else I want raising my children. Finally, I got to pull the ring box out of my jacket pocket, get down on one knee and ask her to give me the honor of being my wife. She was stunned! She had no clue. The expression on her face when she first saw the ring will forever be engrained in my mind. She said yes! Afterwards she told me she couldn't figure out why I was talking so much and not posing for the picture until I popped the question! The rest of the trip was amazing. She loves the ring so much she sleeps in it! Thanks Rick. You helped make both our dreams come true!

SPARKS FLYING!
John & Megan

Four years had passed, and I knew that it was finally time to start the hunt for the perfect ring to propose to my girlfriend, Megan. After talking to all of my buddies about finding a ring, most knew nothing about jewelry, but one of them recommended that I visit Uptown Diamond. I made an appointment to meet Rick, and immediately felt at home walking in the door. Rick educated me about diamonds and helped me pick the perfect one for Megan.

He asked me how I was going to pop the question. I just figured I would do the regular dinner proposal, but knowing that I was a Houston Firefighter, Rick suggested I propose to Megan at the fire station. I took his advice and started planning. As soon as I put the bug into the ears of the rest of the crew, they just took off with it! We came up with the idea of setting up the ladder truck and inviting her to a *Family Day* at the station. The entire district came over for the *Family Day* and we had fire trucks everywhere just waiting for the big moment. Naturally my fiancée wondered where all the families were, so I told Megan that she was there early and she bought it!

The men lined the roof of the truck, and I convinced Megan to follow me across the ladder, where I planned to surprise her with the ring I had been hiding for months. Our song started playing, the American flag was waving in the background and the weather was perfect. As soon as she saw me on one knee I could see tears of joy streaming down her face, and I knew that I had done well. It couldn't have worked out any better.

THE CONAN CONNECTION
Nick & Dilara

Dilara and I had been dating for eighteen months and as odd as it sounds, Conan O'Brien and his show CONAN, had been a constant in our relationship. It all started when we first met and I told her that I was going to be in a sketch on the show the following week. She thought it was a line … and it was, but nevertheless she agreed to go on a proper date with me the following week, which became the start of our relationship.

A few months and a bunch of dates later, I got cast as the lead of a sketch on CONAN called *Gold4Gold*. It was a pretty big deal. The staff at CONAN gave me two seats to the taping and the only person I wanted to bring with me was Dilara. As the show started, I got pretty nervous and didn't even realize that I was squeezing her hand way too hard. She told me to *calm down, dummy* and I did. The sketch aired, the audience loved it and I looked at Dilara, who was beaming with pride and slight embarrassment and I knew at that moment that I wanted to be with her forever.

Dilara got a job at The Pete Holmes Show (which Conan produced) as a graphic designer. On her first day, I was creating another sketch right next door. Five months later during her last day at The Pete Holmes Show, she got to watch me perform my first live sketch while hanging out in the Green Room with Ice Cube. Just to clarify things, Ice Cube plays no part in our relationship going further, I just wanted to brag a little.

While Dilara was at The Pete Holmes Show, they asked her if she ever did any animation. Even though she had very little experience, she said yes, but her natural talent grew and led her to making some incredible animations for the show. The quality of her work soon spread to the offices of Team Coco, Conan's digital arm, and they employed her to make some animations for their website. This led to Conan himself watching her work, and he loved it so much that he put her cartoon ON AIR. He even mentioned her name before the start of the piece, something he rarely does. Now she is currently working on three more animations. So it's safe to say that Conan had a big part of our lives. When I got the ring, I had to figure out a great place to propose, somewhere important, somewhere that really means something to us. I got down to thinking and I came up with two possible places: Conan's stage OR the terrible dive bar where we met. I went with Conan.

I had Vana, a good friend at the show call Dilara in for a *big meeting* which prompted Dilara to freak out and think about all the implications this meeting could have for her career. She immediately went shopping, bought a new outfit for the meeting and updated her portfolio, all while thinking *what could this meeting be about?* I really hoped my proposal would soften the blow of there being no real meeting. Her *meeting* was set for four, and I got there an hour before to get ready. I spent that hour pacing back and forth and talking to Richard Dreyfuss. Suddenly, I got a text from Vana that she was walking up to the stage. It was go time! A minute later she turned the corner at the other end of the stage, and with a look of confusion said, "What are you doing here?" Then she saw the photographer and it hit her. I walked up to her, apologized about there being no actual meeting, got down on one knee, and she said, "Of course dummy." It was the best moment of my life!

BASEBALL DIAMOND
Brooke & Chason

April 26th, 2014 is a day I will never forget! After weeks of secretly planning a surprise birthday party for my boyfriend Chason, the day had finally arrived. Both of us were super excited. After a large breakfast and a brief power nap it was time to unveil the afternoon's festivities. I handed Chason a bag. Inside the bag were two matching T-Shirts, one for each of us. Wondering why I had just handed him two matching T-Shirts, I held up his bag of softball gear and said, "That's what we're wearing today and we need to take this gear with us." Still feeling confused, Chason and I changed into our matching shirts and headed out. We arrived at a bus station where some of our friends were waiting for us. The bus then took the group to Spring, which added even more confusion to the day! Upon arrival at our destination we were welcomed by more friends and family. At this point it became obvious, Chason's big birthday party surprise was a SURPRISE SOFTBALL TOURNAMENT with friends and family!

Chason's team won, of course! After the first game we all went out on the field for a group picture of the rival teams. After taking a few pictures, Chason grabbed my hand and pulled me to the front. I didn't think anything of it, he was just telling everyone thank you for coming and thanked me for pulling it all together. Then he said, "Well, I didn't know we would be on a softball field." He grabbed both of my hands, told me how much he loved me, got down on one knee, pulled out an amazing ring and proposed to me! It was the most perfect, completely unexpected moment of my life! I thought I was surprising him for his birthday! What a surprise I got, the best day of my life, so far! I get to marry my best friend! Thank you Uptown Diamond! My ring couldn't be more gorgeous, it's absolutely perfect!

FRIENDSHIP TURNED LOVE CONNECTION
Jim & Jackie

It's often noted that the greatest love stories began as friendships, and Jim and Jackie certainly embody this sentiment. The two became acquainted twenty-nine years ago through work, and witnessed each other's joys and sorrows throughout the years. This initially led to a solid friendship, and eventually to an unexpected relationship that soon blossomed into LOVE! The couple was devastated when a year into their courtship, Jim was diagnosed with stage 4 prostate cancer. Enduring a year of aggressive chemotherapy and an additional six months of radiation therapy, Jim was blessed to receive Jackie's steadfast support throughout his treatment.

Miraculously, Jim was eventually given the unbelievable news that he was cancer free. His doctors performed a cutting-edge treatment with him that proved to be successful. They were asked to be on *Great Day Houston* and to invite their *star* patients. Jim, a private person by nature, was asked to participate and after reluctantly agreeing to do so, he decided to use the show as a platform to ask for Jackie's hand...on LIVE TV!

Great Day Houston host, Deborah Duncan worked closely with Jim to plan the whole surprise event. On June 8, 2012, Jim was the first guest on that day's show. After giving an inspiring interview, Deborah led into how Jim would want to thank not only his doctors for getting his life back, but also recognize Jackie as well. Jim suddenly came down off the stage and walked into the audience, where Jackie was seated in the front row. In a beautiful moment and before all of Houston, Jim bent down on his knees and asked Jackie to be his wife.

Jackie was totally caught off guard and completely overcome with joy. She said YES! The segment of the show ended with the pair kissing and crying with joy. Afterwards they celebrated with a beautiful lunch at Tony's and began to plan their wedding. Because the engagement was planned very quickly, Jim did not have an opportunity to get an engagement ring. They called Uptown Diamond's Rick Antona to help bring the couple's ring design to life.

After months of planning, the wedding day arrived. The ceremony was held at the First Presbyterian Church in Tomball, TX. In light of Jim's Scottish ancestry, they incorporated many Scottish traditions into the wedding ceremony. Jim and the groomsmen all wore the traditional Scottish kilt. Guests were treated to the soothing hymn of a bagpipe, as well as to readings of the Scottish poet Robbie Burns. Since Jim is also a faithful Beatle's fan, Jackie enlisted musicians to re-enact a scene from the movie *Love Actually*. As the couple walked down the aisle for the first time as man and wife, the musicians popped up and serenaded the congregation with the famous song, *All You Need Is Love.*

NAPA VALLEY SURPRISE
Griffin & Holly

We took a group trip to Napa Valley with ten of our friends. Early Friday morning, Holly and I went on a private hot air balloon ride. It was just the two of us (and the pilot) on the flight. We launched at about 7:00 a.m. When we reached an altitude of 3,000 feet, I asked

Holly to search in my backpack and grab the GoPro camera out of the case so we could take some videos. When she opened the GoPro case, the engagement ring was hiding inside. I got down on one knee in the hot air balloon and asked her to marry me, and of course, she said, "Yes!"

After the hot air balloon landed, we drove back to the house we were staying. Both of our families were waiting there to surprise her. We all took a bus together to Cindy's Backstreet Kitchen for lunch, followed by a special tour of two different wineries, *Pride Mountain* and *BCellars*. To round out the evening, we enjoyed a delicious four-course dinner prepared for the two of us by a private chef back at the house. It was an amazing, unforgettable day. One for the books!

GLOSSARY OF TERMS

AGS: The American Gem Society is the country's preeminent jewelry trade organization dedicated to consumer protection. www.americangemsociety.org

Bearding: A possible blemish on the edges of a diamond that appears as hairline fractures.

Blemish: A flaw on the exterior of the diamond (a scratch, abrasion, nick or chip).

Bonded: A natural diamond that is fully warranted by a jeweler (covers breakage, buy back and exchange).

Brilliance: White light that is reflected back from a diamond.

Brilliant: A round diamond with 58 facets.

Carat: A unit of weight equal to 200 milligrams.

Carbon: The raw material that diamonds are made from. Occasionally a diamond will have a minute pocket of carbon that appears as a black spot in the stone.

Chip: Wear and tear during the cutting process which could cause small pieces of the diamond to fall out.

Clarity: A gem's degree of flawlessness.

Cloud: A Cluster of small inclusions or internal flaws that are inside the diamond.

Coatings: A non-permanent process that adds a thin film of synthetic diamond to a diamond simulant, giving it many of the characteristics of a real diamond.

Color: The diamond's body color or its absence of color.

Crown: The bottom facet of a diamond.

Crystal: White spots.

Culet: Located at the very bottom tip of a diamond, the purpose of the culet, a small flat facet is to protect the diamond. Diamond settings typically protect the pavilion of the stone from daily wear.

Cut: The proportion of the stone.

Dispersion: Colored light reflected from within the diamond, also referred to as fire.

Eye-clean: A diamond with no inclusions and/or blemishes that can be seen by the naked eye.

Facet: A polished surface on a diamond.

Feather: Any kind of fissure within a diamond.

Fire: Flashes of prismatic color created by the dispersion of light.

Fluorescence: A diamond's reaction to ultraviolet (UV) light which causes the stone to glow in various colors.

Fracture: A true crack on the surface of the diamond, larger than bearding.

Fracture Filling: A process where a glass-like substance is injected into narrow fractures or cracks of an imperfect diamond.

Gemologist: Someone trained and accredited in diamonds and colored stones.

GIA: Gemological Institute of America (GIA) is a nonprofit gem research institute dedicated to provide corporate & company gem education in the field of gemology & jewelry arts. **www.gia.edu**

Girdle: The narrow, unpolished or faceted band around the widest part of the diamond. The girdle separates the crown and the pavilion of the stone.

Head: Prongs that hold a diamond in its setting.

Heating/HPHT: A process that alters lower class diamonds through heat and pressure applications.

Inclusion: A flaw within a diamond, (carbon spots or fractures).

Irradiation: A high energy process that physically alters the diamond's crystalline structure.

Karat: The measure of the purity of gold with 24-karat being pure gold. Jewelry is typically made from 18k or 14k gold. It contains other metals to make it stronger.

Lapidarist: A skilled diamond cutter.

Laser-drilled: A diamond treated with a laser to remove carbon spots or other inclusions.

Loupe: A small magnifying glass used to examine gemstones (should be minimum 10x magnification).

Megascope: A machine that is used to evaluate a stone's properties such as its proportions and symmetry. Similar to a Sarin.

Natural: Unpolished diamond (or parts of a diamond).

Pavilion: Everything below the diamond's girdle—the bottom of a diamond.

Pinpoint: Very small spots or tiny internal dots.

Point: 1/100th of a carat. A diamond weighing 1.0 carats would be 100 points.

Polishing Lines: A mistake made manually that causes minute lines on the diamond during the polishing process.

Roughs: Diamonds in their untouched state.

Sarin: A Sarin scan uses lasers evaluate stone's proportions and symmetry. It can reveal subtle problems within a stone. Similar to a Megascope.

Scintillation: The intense sparkle effect that a diamond produces. It is the contrasting darkness and lightness alternates from one facet to the next to makes the diamond sparkle.

Scratch: Seen typically as a line on the diamond that tarnishes its smooth surface.

Semi-mount: A setting that is complete except it is missing the main stone which is selected separately.

Single-cut: A diamond with only 16 or 17 facets.

Sparkle: The way the light reflects on the diamond because of way the brilliance and the fire disperse.

Table: The largest facet on a diamond located at the flat top where the light enters and exits.

Tiffany: A 203 mm ring setting that is simple and elegant, with a head that holds a single diamond.

Twinning Wisp: A series of pinpoints, clouds or crystals that often appear as a ripple or a wispy line. These are formed during the diamond's development produced by an irregularity in the crystal structure.

DIAMOND NOTES

*Use this section to take notes as you search
for your perfect diamond.*

DIAMOND NOTES

DIAMOND NOTES

DIAMOND NOTES

DIAMOND NOTES

DIAMOND NOTES

DIAMOND NOTES

DIAMOND NOTES

DIAMOND NOTES

DIAMOND NOTES

DIAMOND NOTES

DIAMOND NOTES

DIAMOND NOTES

www.ingramcontent.com/pod-product-compliance
Lightning Source LLC
Chambersburg PA
CBHW060502280326
41933CB00014B/2835